CONTENTS

Published By Century Books Limted,
Unit I, Upside Station Building, Solsbro Road,
Torquay, Devon. TQ2 6FD.
books@centurybooksltd.co.uk   Published 2012

www.justinbiebermusic.com
www.justinbieberstore.com
www.justinbiebermusic.com/justforyou

£6.99

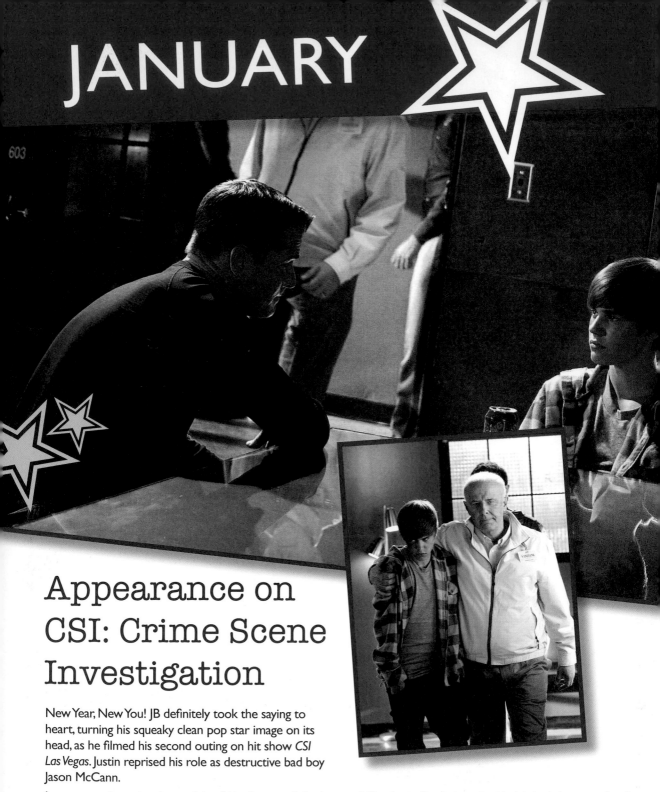

JANUARY

Appearance on CSI: Crime Scene Investigation

New Year, New You! JB definitely took the saying to heart, turning his squeaky clean pop star image on its head, as he filmed his second outing on hit show *CSI Las Vegas*. Justin reprised his role as destructive bad boy Jason McCann.

In an on-set interview he explained his character's background, "I'm basically playing a bad kid, I don't have any family, I'm raised by this guy named Dr. Huxbee who beats me, I really hate the government and I'm trying to bomb the LVPD [Las Vegas Police Department]. It's pretty crazy. I don't care about anything — they killed my brother and I act like I care but really I couldn't care less, I just want to blow them up."

JUSTIN BIEBER

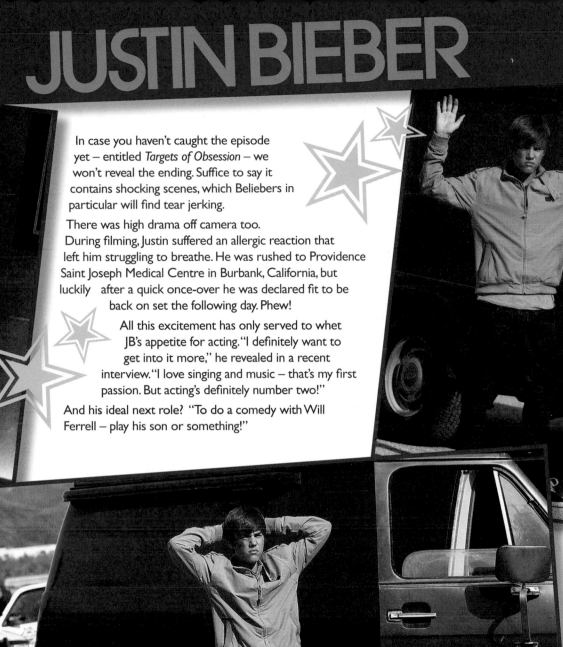

In case you haven't caught the episode yet – entitled *Targets of Obsession* – we won't reveal the ending. Suffice to say it contains shocking scenes, which Beliebers in particular will find tear jerking.

There was high drama off camera too. During filming, Justin suffered an allergic reaction that left him struggling to breathe. He was rushed to Providence Saint Joseph Medical Centre in Burbank, California, but luckily after a quick once-over he was declared fit to be back on set the following day. Phew!

All this excitement has only served to whet JB's appetite for acting. "I definitely want to get into it more," he revealed in a recent interview. "I love singing and music – that's my first passion. But acting's definitely number two!"

And his ideal next role? "To do a comedy with Will Ferrell – play his son or something!"

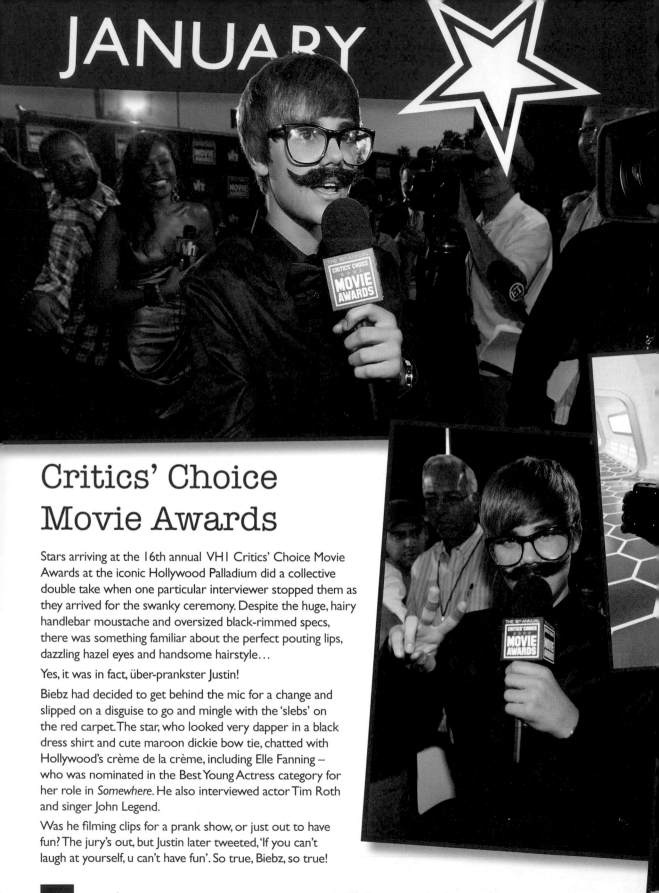

Critics' Choice Movie Awards

Stars arriving at the 16th annual VH1 Critics' Choice Movie Awards at the iconic Hollywood Palladium did a collective double take when one particular interviewer stopped them as they arrived for the swanky ceremony. Despite the huge, hairy handlebar moustache and oversized black-rimmed specs, there was something familiar about the perfect pouting lips, dazzling hazel eyes and handsome hairstyle...

Yes, it was in fact, über-prankster Justin!

Biebz had decided to get behind the mic for a change and slipped on a disguise to go and mingle with the 'slebs' on the red carpet. The star, who looked very dapper in a black dress shirt and cute maroon dickie bow tie, chatted with Hollywood's crème de la crème, including Elle Fanning – who was nominated in the Best Young Actress category for her role in *Somewhere*. He also interviewed actor Tim Roth and singer John Legend.

Was he filming clips for a prank show, or just out to have fun? The jury's out, but Justin later tweeted, 'If you can't laugh at yourself, u can't have fun'. So true, Biebz, so true!

JUSTIN BIEBER

'Big Game' Commericial

JB flexed his comedy muscle again this month, when he headed to Universal Studios in LA to shoot a commercial to run during the Super Bowl.

The advertisement was for US electrical retailer Best Buy. The concept – that technology moves fast so you need a store that will make sure you don't get left behind – was given a hilarious spin with the inspired casting of rock veteran Ozzy Osbourne alongside a new generation of pop star – Justin Biebz.

In the ad, Ozzy struggles to deliver his lines about a new 5G phone. The director then replaces him with Justin who shows off an even cooler phone saying, "It's Bieber, 6G Fever!" before wowing the camera with some robotic dance moves. Sharon Osbourne, looking on, asks her hubbie, "What's a 6G?" and Ozzie replies, "What's a Bieber?" The brilliant punch line comes from Biebz, disguised as a member of the film crew who replies, "Dunno… kinda looks like a girl!"

Chillin' @ the basketball

JB seemed to be channelling his inner Smurf when he showed up at an NBA basketball game in Atlanta to watch the Atlanta Hawks play the New Orleans Hornets. The star looked cute but kinda kooky in grey jeans, black-framed glasses, a yellow zipped hoody and a sky blue beanie. Luckily Justin can carry off any look without even trying! There was also a practical element to his outfit – those knitted fingerless gloves must have come in handy when handling his freezing tub of ice cream!

JANUARY

Golden Globe Awards

Biebz had some competition for the hottest hunk in Hollywood when he showed up on the red carpet at the 2011 Golden Globe Awards at the Beverly Hilton Hotel. He brushed tux-clad shoulders with the likes of RPatz, Zac Efron and The Jonas Bros!

He totally held his own however, looking pin sharp in a black satin tuxedo, white shirt and black skinny tie by D&G. Biebz added his own unique touches, too – a blinging titanium black diamond ring by David Yurman and a cool pair of white-soled trainers.

Biebz would have course have looked just as hot in a sack – and he could have worn one for all the attention his outfit got – as the eyes of the world's media were firmly trained on his new hairdo. Gone was the trademark mop top; in its place an even cooler crop.

After cosying up to Angelina Jolie, Biebz joined Jon M. Chu – director of his movie Justin Bieber – Never Say Never 3D – for an interview with Ryan Seacrest. The E! presenter asked JB how he even found the time to attend events like the Globes and the star's honest reply was, "They put it in my schedule so I mean, I just kind of showed up!" He and Jon Chu went on to talk about the film, with Jon describing the inspirational story as "a fairy-tale for this generation."

Once inside, Justin's work really started. He presented the Best Animated Movie Award to Toy Story 3 alongside True Grit star Hailee Steinfeld. What a night!

The Late Show with David Letterman

As part of the promotional tour for *Never Say Never*, Justin appeared on David Letterman's hit US talk show. Always the gentleman, he signed autographs for fans before going in, charming a lucky guest when he presented her with some Belgian waffles.

In the interview the cheeky chappy revealed a tux-printed T-shirt and told the host, "I dressed up for you". He then got out his mobile and tweeted, 'I'm just hanging out with my boy Dave!'

The pair chatted about the fact Justin only drives in Canada, but not in busy cities like New York, before going on to discuss JB's musical influences, his family and the movie.

"I wanted to let people know I'm not some factory machine put together by other people," said Justin afterwards.

The 'Never Say Never' Remix Release

On 25th January, Justin's awesome track 'Never say Never' featuring Jaden Smith was released as the lead single from his forthcoming album, 'Never Say Never – The Remixes'. The song had originally been made available to download the previous summer, debuting in the top 40 on the Billboard 100 Chart and climbing to number 8, so it was certain to be even more in demand with the film release just around the corner.

The cool music video was directed by Honey, the visionary behind the clips to Ke$ha's 'Your Love Is My Drug' and KT Tunstall's 'Suddenly I See'. It featured Biebz and pal Jaden clad in leather jackets and hi-top trainers, laying down the track in the recording studio. These segments were intercut with scenes from the film *Karate Kid*, starring Jaden as Dre Parker.

B provided the main vocals with 'J Smith' or 'lil bro' as Biebz calls him – pulling off a sick rap! Of course it wasn't all work and no play for the pair, who quickly became firm friends. The boys had a great time fooling around and showing off their dance moves. One clip showed them dancin' together. They also shadowboxed and wrestled at the mixing desk. Biebz even got in on the martial arts action – performing a perfect spinning roundhouse kick at the end.

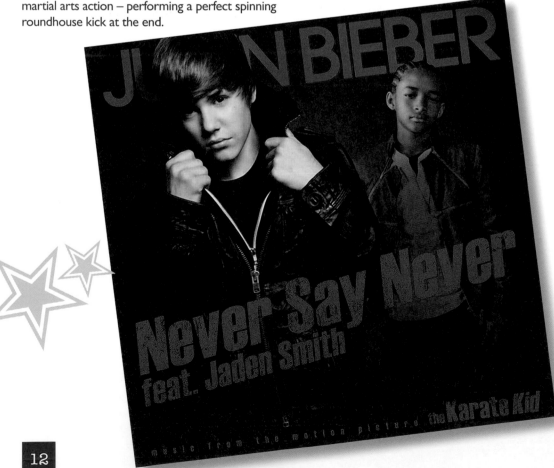

JUSTIN BIEBER

Tweets of the month

@ Backstage at the Golden Globes. Everyone is here. This is nuts!! Halle Berry was at my table. #badass. De Niro is the man.

@ Met at the Globes and she is super talented. CONGRATS to Hailee Steinfeld for being 14 and getting nominated for an OSCAR for TRUE GRIT!

@ RANDOM CHUCK NORRIS MOMENT: The reason it rains is CHUCK NORRIS scared the clouds, and they wet themselves. #fact.

@ Just heard someone request NEVER SAY NEVER on the radio. very cool. Thanks for the love. much appreciated.

@ I'm hanging out with my boy Dave at @late_show we need to get him twice as many followers! #justdoit.

@ Glad to have @taylorswift13 as a friend. Everyone should be as nice as her!

Justin Bieber – Never Say Never 3D The Movie

So finally the moment dawned.

Beliebers around the world flocked in their millions to the cinema for the first glimpse of their idol on the silver screen and they weren't disappointed.

The film, directed by Jon M. Chu, the guru behind brilliant movies like *Step Up 2: The Streets* and *Step Up 3D*, has a documentary feel. It follows JB around during the ten days leading up to his August 2010 sellout concert at New York's Madison Square Garden. All-access footage from the concerts, rehearsals and backstage footage are combined with the endearing rags to riches back-story of the talented music prodigy who came to the attention of an agent via YouTube. The inspirational and uplifting story quickly captured the hearts of audiences around the world.

The film was a box office smash. Having cost around $13 million to make (which is actually not very much in movie terms), it took almost $30 million on its opening weekend in the USA alone. It has since gone on to make over $98 million worldwide.

Jon Chu said the idea was to make the film's plot "like a hyperlink", so unlike other concert films which show only music and backstage action, it would tell the tale of Justin's incredible career, and set stories from his life to a soundtrack of his own music.

The heartwarming movie includes many honest, personal moments from Justin's childhood, growing up with his mother Pattie Mallette and maternal grandparents Bruce and Diane Dale. There's also footage showing the difficulties JB faces combining his home-life with his career as a pop superstar. In one section of the film Biebz goes home to Canada and hangs out with his pals, only to be scolded by his voice coach Jan when he gets back because he has damaged his vocal chords through yelling and laughing with his friends.

The film also includes scenes showing JB indulging in one of his favourite pastimes – pranking! The naughty boy loves playing tricks on his crew, his friends and his family. Biebz said his motivation in doing the film was, "to let people know [that] there's a lot of people that are discouraging in life and that will tell you that you can't do something, but you just got to remember that the sky's the limit. You're able to do whatever you set your mind to as long as you remember to keep God first and stay grounded. So, I think the movie really explains that, and it's really inspiring."

On seeing the movie, even the Bieber haters had to admit defeat, with one normally savage critic admitting that, "as a 3D glimpse of a building pop culture phenomenon, *Never Say Never* is undeniably entertaining."

The build-up to the release was epic, with Jon Chu announcing a contest where people could upload clips of themselves performing 'That Should Be Me' or 'U Smile' to JB's official fan club website, BieberFever.com. There was another contest where fans were sent on a scavenger hunt online to try and piece together the name of the forthcoming movie using clues given by celebs such as Usher, actress Ellen DeGeneres and presenter Ryan Seacrest.

Los Angeles Première of Never Say Never

Could anything really top the premières in Toronto and New York? From a celebrity point of view the LA opening bash was unbeatable. The purple-themed event at the Nokia Theatre was rammed with stars, literally! The guest list read like a who's who of Hollywood talent.

From the world of music came Miley Cyrus – accompanied by mum Tish and little sister Noah, plus Leona Lewis, Will.i.am, Sean Kingston and Usher. These a-listers jostled for space on the red carpet with young actors and actresses including The Hills star Whitney Port, Suite Life of Zac and Cody regular Debby Ryan and of course Wizards of Waverly Place star Selena Gomez, who looked incredible in a purple satin dress. Jaden Smith turned up with his entire family – Mum Jada, Dad Will and 'Whip My Hair' sister Willow.

Biebz suited up smart in a purple velvet tux with satin lapels and seemed totally awestruck by the huge turnout. Interviewed on the red carpet he gushed, "This is amazing! Everyone's here for me! It's out of control."

London Première of Never Say Never

JB and the crew then took Bieber Fever to the UK, heading to London for the European Première of *Never Say Never*, which was showcased at Greenwich's massive O² Arena.

Justin dressed like a city gent for the occasion in head to toe Dolce & Gabbana togs. With his usual flair for mixing formal and laid-back styles he sported a natty black waistcoat and cute bow tie with a white shirt and distressed jeans and trainers. Arriving by limo, the star was greeted by legions of screaming fans, many of whom had camped out overnight hoping to get a glimpse of the star – or better still a free ticket to the screening.

JB blew kisses and signed autographs, thanking his "amazing and supportive fans" and declaring he wished he "could let them all in."

Despite the cold February weather, British stars who turned out to support the Biebz included Alesha Dixon, Craig David and Jessie J who declared herself "a Bieber Diva" explaining, "I'm a supporter of people that work hard and he's definitely that."

Once inside, Biebz chowed down on a massive tray of nachos and guacamole choosing to wash it down with an electric blue-coloured slushie drink. Brain Freeze!

FEBRUARY

53rd GRAMMY Awards

It was 'all white on the night' for JB when he attended America's biggest annual music awards, the GRAMMYs.

OK, so Biebz, who wore a fab white tuxedo suit, was pipped at the post for the Best New Artist award by American jazz bassist and singer Esperanza Spalding, and also lost out to Lady Gaga in the Best Pop Vocal Album category. But the star was in great spirits and was very gracious about losing, congratulating his rivals backstage and vowing later, "to work harder next year."

Backstage, JB hung out with the brilliant Rihanna dressed in a stunning white ruffled Jean Paul Gaultier mermaid gown. He also rubbed shoulders with singer Cee Lo Green who was turning heads in an eye-popping multi-coloured costume.

On Stage At The GRAMMYs

During the show Biebz got to prove to the audience and the millions of viewers exactly why he deserved to be nominated for such mammoth awards. Big screens around the auditorium showed clips of his first performance for Usher as a nervous 13-year-old, before JB and his mentor appeared on stage.

Justin gave a great acoustic performance of 'Baby' then was joined by Jaden Smith for a rocking rendition of 'Never Say Never'. Finally, he and Usher duetted on 'O.M.G.' Just, wow!

All-Star Basketball Event

Biebz is a dedicated sports fan – watching or playing, he doesn't mind which. As basketball is one of his favourite sports, he was delighted to be invited to take part in the BBVA All-Star celebrity basketball game at the NBA All-Star Weekend in LA!

Wearing a red vest emblazoned with the LA All-Stars logo, the player number 6 and sporting canary yellow Adidas hi-tops, Justin looked totally at home playing alongside towering NBA legends like Scottie Pippen. The star proved himself to be a powerhouse on court, nipping in and out of players, passing cleverly and setting up several awesome shots for his team which was coached by the legendary Magic Johnson.

At the final whistle Justin had scored eight points, got two rebounds and four assists. His obvious skill surprised his opponents and delighted spectators with one announcer saying, "Justin Bieber! He should be thinking about that Most Valued Player award. He has game!" Tru Dat!

Perhaps unsurprisingly, due to his outstanding performance – and tweeting fans to summon votes – the Biebz was awarded the MVP trophy at the end of the contest. Beaming, he accepted the award saying, "We're just out here having a good time!" Is there anything the boy wonder can't do?

JUSTIN BIEBER

FEBRUARY

The Brit Awards

The UK showed its love for Biebz with a Valentine's gift to remember in the shape of a coveted Brit Award. Justin beat off stiff competition to scoop the gong for International Breakthrough Artist.

He was presented with the award by singer Will Young and fellow Canadian Avril Lavigne. Justin even got a congratulatory kiss from Cheryl Cole, who was sitting at the next table.

Knicks Basketball

Biebz rounded off a great month at the NBA All-Star Basketball Game at the Staples Center in LA.

Sandwiched between Rihanna, who was performing at the event, and Beyoncé, JB had the best seat in the house! Ri-Ri giggled as JB showed her something funny on his phone and then it was Beyoncé's turn to laugh, as Chicago Bulls mascot Benny the Bull ruffled Justin's hair-do.

Tweets of the month

@ Sitting here in the Toronto première with fans friends and family. #home – it's a great feeling. Thank you.

@ Now getting ready for NYC première for #NEVERSAYNEVER3D …my guy LA REID told me he is bringing a special guest.

@ UK fans!!! Heads up… rumors are true… the team wIll be giving out tickets to random fans at the O2 today for the #NSN3D premiere 2nite!

@ Everyone text 'bieber' to 69622 for me to be MVP in the all-star celeb game. I'm going in!!! Haha.

@ Tonight was a great night. I got to perform at the Grammys with my mentor Usher Raymond IV and I feel like we did you guys proud. As for the awards… of course I wanted to win. It's been and still is a dream to win a Grammy. Was I upset…? Yes. But I was happy for her, also someone said to me tonight it's not your successes that define u but your failures. I lost…. but I don't plan on this being my last chance… I do this because I love it… and I do it for my family, friends and fans who support me. I was grateful for the honour and this is just the beginning.

Tour Dates: UK, Ireland and Europe

March 4	Birmingham	UK	NIA
March 5	Birmingham	UK	NIA
March 8	Dublin	IRELAND	The O^2
March 9	Dublin	IRELAND	The O^2
March 11	Liverpool	UK	Echo Arena
March 12	Newcastle	UK	Metro Arena
March 14	London	UK	O^2 Arena
March 16	London	UK	O^2 Arena
March 17	London	UK	O^2 Arena
March 20	Manchester	UK	MEN Arena
March 21	Manchester	UK	MEN Arena
March 23	Sheffield	UK	Motorpoint Arena
March 24	Nottingham	UK	Trent FM Arena
March 26	Oberhausen	GERMANY	Konig Pilsener Arena
March 29	Paris	FRANCE	Palais Omnisports de Paris-Bercy
March 30	Antwerp	BELGIUM	Sportpaleis Antwerp

On Tour in Birmingham

March began with a bang, seeing Biebz jetting in to Heathrow to kick off the UK leg of his 'My World' concert tour.

The magic started in Birmingham with two sell-out dates at the NIA arena. Thousands of screaming fans were treated to JB's full repertoire, performed with a dazzling array of costumes including a silver suit and a red leather jacket. Biebz also showed off his musical skills by playing the guitar and doing a fantastic drum solo.

Justin made sure that as many of his British fans as possible got to see him, with dates in seven major cities plus two dates in Dublin, Ireland.

On Stage With Willow Smith

Jaden Smith's little sis' Willow joined JB for the UK and Ireland legs of the tour. The star opened each show for Justin, performing her smash hits 'I Whip My Hair' and '21st Century Girl' to screaming fans. Willow was of course accompanied by her parents Will and Jada and her big bro, who were there to cheer her on at every gig.

Poor Willow fell victim to the Biebz's legendary love for pranks while opening the Manchester show. JB, Scooter and Bieber's swagger coach, Ryan Good, stormed the stage dressed as female backing dancers. Scooter and Ryan whipped their fake wigs along to the lyrics!

Off-stage Willow and Justin had a ball. Whenever they had some downtime they took in the sights, ate out at great local restaurants and shopped up a storm. They even brought über toy-store Hamleys on Regent Street to a near standstill during the London leg of the tour.

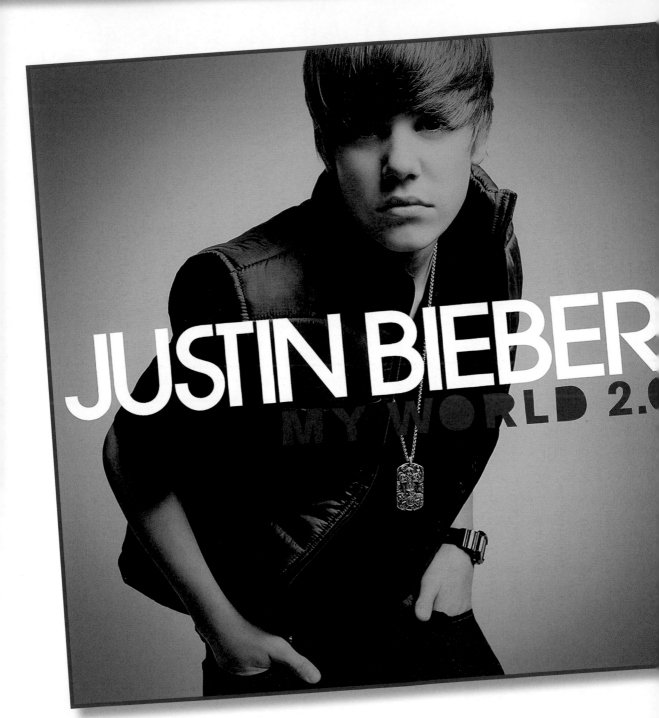

'My World 2.0' Album Release

The fans had waited long enough. Finally on 19th March their patience paid off when Biebz released 'My World 2.0'. The second part of his debut release has been recorded during the same studio sessions as the tracks on 'My World', but Justin had so much great material he'd decided to split it over two albums so the fans wouldn't have to wait too long for new music from him.

Justin worked with cool producers such as Tricky Stewart, The-Dream and The Stereotypes to give the album an edgier, more mature feel.

"I wanted to do something that was a little bit more R&B and that could reach out to everyone. I just wanted to be able to show my vocal abilities," the star said in an interview at the time.

JB also talked about how his lyric-writing abilities are evolving and developing. "I think I am growing up and that the lyrics show that… I want to sing about things that are going on in my life, and a lot of people will be able to relate to it."

Biebz was spot on. Fans related to such a degree that the album debuted at number one on the U.S. Billboard 200, shifting over 283,000 copies in its first week and making Justin the youngest solo male act to top the chart since Stevie Wonder in 1963! He also became the first artist to occupy two top five spots on the chart since 2004.

Amazingly, after such a huge initial sales rush, the album's sales continued to rise. This is virtually unheard of, making Biebz the first act since sixties group The Beatles to debut at number one and sell more the following week.

The ten tracks on the album included several clever collaborations - in particular the smash hit 'Baby' — pre-released in January. This unbelievably catchy track featured rapper Ludacris and reached the top ten in fifteen countries worldwide. The video, which was shot in a bowling alley by director Ray Kay and featured singer and actress Jasmine Villegas, became the most watched YouTube video of the year with 408 million views.

Biebz also collaborated with Sean Kingston on 'Eenie Meenie'. The pair shared vocals and larked about in the video clip, which saw them vying for the attention of a cute girl at a pool party. As usual Biebz worked incredibly hard to promote his work doing hundreds of media interviews, personal appearances and meet and greets with fans. He even threw a release party called *Bowling with Bieber* in conjunction with New York-based radio station 92.3 NOW. Fans competed to win tickets to visit the Lucky Strike Lanes bowling alley in Manhattan where they would meet Justin and get to hear the album. Ever the sportsman, Biebz destroyed radio host Nick Cannon in his match!

'My World 2.0' also trended majorly on Twitter, becoming the second most talked about topic in the Twitterverse, with tweeters in their millions announcing that they were listening to the album.

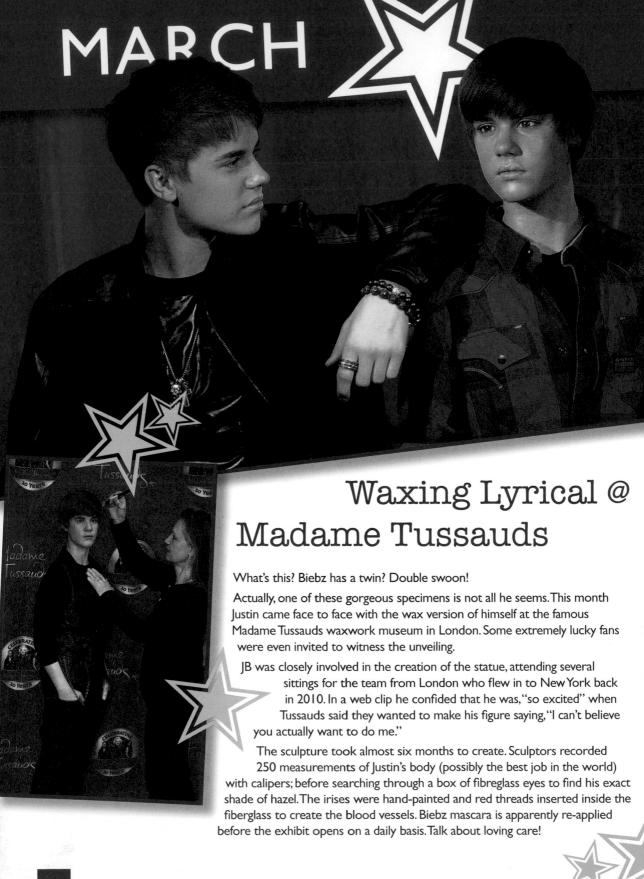

Waxing Lyrical @ Madame Tussauds

What's this? Biebz has a twin? Double swoon!

Actually, one of these gorgeous specimens is not all he seems. This month Justin came face to face with the wax version of himself at the famous Madame Tussauds waxwork museum in London. Some extremely lucky fans were even invited to witness the unveiling.

JB was closely involved in the creation of the statue, attending several sittings for the team from London who flew in to New York back in 2010. In a web clip he confided that he was, "so excited" when Tussauds said they wanted to make his figure saying, "I can't believe you actually want to do me."

The sculpture took almost six months to create. Sculptors recorded 250 measurements of Justin's body (possibly the best job in the world) with calipers; before searching through a box of fibreglass eyes to find his exact shade of hazel. The irises were hand-painted and red threads inserted inside the fiberglass to create the blood vessels. Biebz mascara is apparently re-applied before the exhibit opens on a daily basis. Talk about loving care!

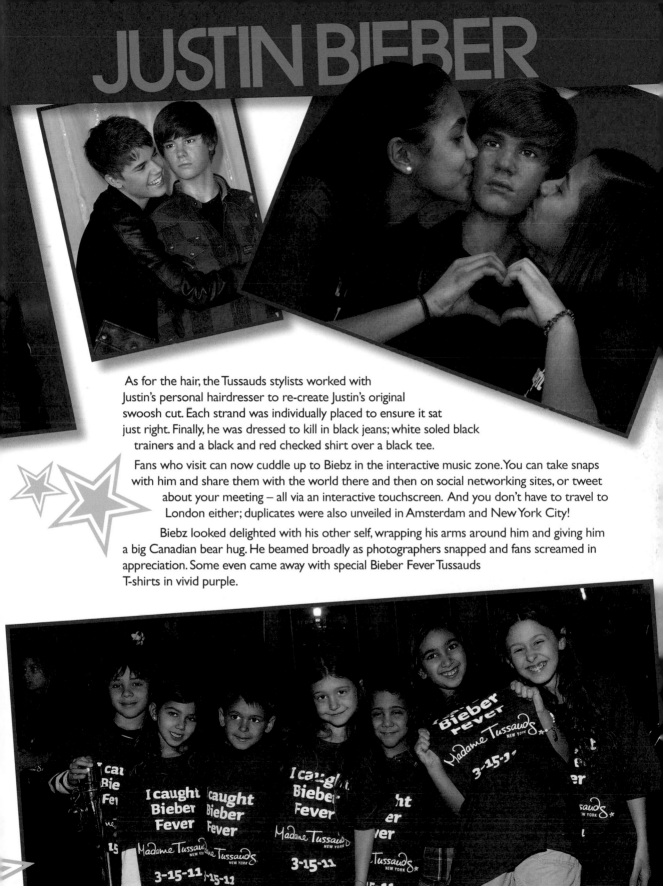

As for the hair, the Tussauds stylists worked with Justin's personal hairdresser to re-create Justin's original swoosh cut. Each strand was individually placed to ensure it sat just right. Finally, he was dressed to kill in black jeans; white soled black trainers and a black and red checked shirt over a black tee.

Fans who visit can now cuddle up to Biebz in the interactive music zone. You can take snaps with him and share them with the world there and then on social networking sites, or tweet about your meeting – all via an interactive touchscreen. And you don't have to travel to London either; duplicates were also unveiled in Amsterdam and New York City!

Biebz looked delighted with his other self, wrapping his arms around him and giving him a big Canadian bear hug. He beamed broadly as photographers snapped and fans screamed in appreciation. Some even came away with special Bieber Fever Tussauds T-shirts in vivid purple.

35

Live On German TV

After his hectic time in the UK, Justin headed to Europe for the remaining dates of his tour. While he was in Germany, the star took time to travel to Augsburg in the South of the country to appear on the country's most popular Saturday game show *Wetten Dass…?* Which means *'Wanna Bet?'*

The host, Thomas Gottschalk, really put JB through the mill, asking him to solve a Rubik's cube puzzle – which he did with ease – and try on an horrendous wig, rather like the host's own bouffant barnet! The obliging star smiled through it all and still found the energy to perform a brilliant medley of 'Pray' and 'Never Say Never' for the excited audience.

Rotterdam Loves Biebz

Gearing up for another night onstage, Justin attended a press conference at the Ahoy Stadium in Rotterdam, Netherlands. A lucky fan got to ask him some questions and just before being ushered off stage, the cheeky minx asked, "What do I have do to get tickets for one of your concerts?" to which JB quipped, "Never say never, right?" Biebz was then presented with a special platinum album award.

Tweets of the month

@ Willow is killing IT in the opening set. Super proud of her and excited for you to see it. Me and Jaden watched like proud big bros.

@ Whatup @chrisbrown – I think our fans might need to team up and start requesting #NEXT2YOU at local radio. #TEAMBREEZY and #TEAMBIEBER = WOW

@ This is crazy. There are like thousands of people out there. Love everybody but gonna try and get some sleep. Please don't scream. lol. [WhIle in Liverpool]

@ AMAZING SHOW 2nite at the O2!! Brought out Craig David which was crazy because I grew up listening to him.

@ Arrived @tussaudslondon to see my WAX figure!! The 1st time I saw a wax figure was in NYC and all we could do was look thro the glass. Now we are here in London and they r about to show my figure here and in Amsterdam and in NYC at the one we looked thru the glass. #DREAMBIG Knew @studiomama had more kids! me and my mom and lil bro.

@ Good morning Rotterdam... time for some school. On a weekend?!

Footy With Barcelona

Justin Bieber can make anything look hot – even the lurid green training kit of super-club Barcelona FC!

While in Spain, Biebz, who is a big fan of the team, visited the club's official training ground in Ciutat Esportiva Joan Gamper. After watching a training session from the bench, JB changed from his grey hoodie into warm-up shorts and tops and took the pitch!

Soon Biebz was having an all-star kick around with top players including striker Bojan Krkic, Benja Martinez, Andreu Fontàs, Thiago Alcântara and goalie Rubén Miño. The star showed off his skills and had several shots at goal.

Before leaving, Biebz told players and the waiting press that he loved playing football in his spare time, describing the opportunity to train at Barcelona, "an honour."

Dolce & Gabbana Party

After performing to capacity crowds at Milan's Mediolanum Forum, Biebz attended a party thrown in his honour by two of his favourite fashion designers, Domenico Dolce and Stefano Gabbana, aka the iconic D&G.

Justin arrived in a limo, greeted outside the club by the designers who looked delighted to see him, each shaking his hands enthusiastically. Justin wore identical black-rimmed specs to theirs – in tribute perhaps – teaming the glasses with a slouchy grey hoody emblazoned with a black and white image of movie idol James Dean.

After posing for pictures together, the trio headed indoors for some real partying. The DJ mixed beats from Rihanna and Usher while Biebz showed off his distinctive dance-floor moves, at one point donning the DJ's hat.

JB frequently sports suits, tuxes and ties from the D&G collections when he goes to parties, award ceremonies and premières. It seems the respect is mutual – Biebz is considered a muse by the fashion designers. Stefano Gabbana recently said, "Justin represents the epitome of the new generation of music talent. We are fascinated by his capability of communicating to a wide variety of audiences, from the teenagers to a more adult public." Domenico Dolce added, "We do love Justin's music. We listened to his last album during our fashion show preparation and in our free time – it's in our playlist! He belongs to the new generation, he cares about fashion. We are very happy to dress him and we admire him a lot."

Tour Dates: Europe, Asia and Australasia

April 1	Herning	DENMARK	Jyske Bank Boxen
April 2	Berlin	GERMANY	O² World Arena
April 5	Madrid	SPAIN	Palacio de Deportes
April 6	Barcelona	SPAIN	Palau Sant Jordi
April 8	Zurich	SWITZERLAND	Hallenstadion
April 9	Milan	ITALY	Mediolanum Forum
April 14	Tel Aviv	ISRAEL	Hayarkon Park
April 19	Singapore	SINGAPORE	Singapore Indoor Stadium
April 21	Kuala Lumpur	MALAYSIA	Stadium Merdeka
April 23	Bogor	INDONESIA	Sentul City ICC
April 26	Brisbane	AUSTRALIA	Brisbane Entertainment Centre
April 28	Sydney	AUSTRALIA	Acer Arena
April 29	Sydney	AUSTRALIA	Acer Arena

JUSTIN BIEBER

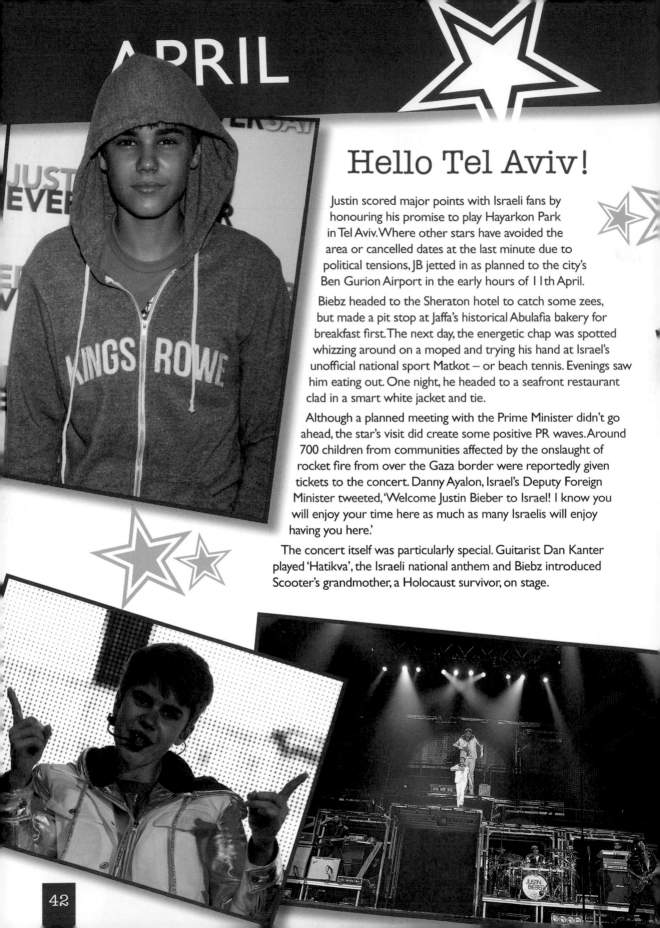

Hello Tel Aviv!

Justin scored major points with Israeli fans by honouring his promise to play Hayarkon Park in Tel Aviv. Where other stars have avoided the area or cancelled dates at the last minute due to political tensions, JB jetted in as planned to the city's Ben Gurion Airport in the early hours of 11th April.

Biebz headed to the Sheraton hotel to catch some zees, but made a pit stop at Jaffa's historical Abulafia bakery for breakfast first. The next day, the energetic chap was spotted whizzing around on a moped and trying his hand at Israel's unofficial national sport Matkot – or beach tennis. Evenings saw him eating out. One night, he headed to a seafront restaurant clad in a smart white jacket and tie.

Although a planned meeting with the Prime Minister didn't go ahead, the star's visit did create some positive PR waves. Around 700 children from communities affected by the onslaught of rocket fire from over the Gaza border were reportedly given tickets to the concert. Danny Ayalon, Israel's Deputy Foreign Minister tweeted, 'Welcome Justin Bieber to Israel! I know you will enjoy your time here as much as many Israelis will enjoy having you here.'

The concert itself was particularly special. Guitarist Dan Kanter played 'Hatikva', the Israeli national anthem and Biebz introduced Scooter's grandmother, a Holocaust survivor, on stage.

JUSTIN BIEBER

Arriving In Singapore

After leaving Israel, Justin really clocked up some air miles! First stop was Singapore, where Biebz took the opportunity to speak to the country's media for the first time. In a pre-gig press conference he really opened up. "I'm sure you have all been 17 years old. You have your insecurities. You are dating girls and trying to figure out who you are, so I am still going through that," he said.

JB was also quick to defend the thing most important to him, his faith, talking of how the paparazzi who had followed him into a church in Israel had "crossed the line."

On a lighter note, Justin told the press he wants to explore a movie career and how he'd love to star opposite Jessica Alba. And, when asked if he could live without Twitter he said, "The fans freak out when I go a day without Twitter, they think I'm dead, so I try to tweet as much as I can." Never stop tweeting Biebz!

JUSTIN BIEBER

Tweets of the month

@ The next Pelé lol jk.
[After training with Barcelona.]

@ Love Italy. Best food ever! Show was incredible and the party was fun. Thanks for the good times. Now off to Israel!

@ AMAZING NIGHT… AMAZING PLACE… AMAZING SHOW!!
NEVER GOING TO FORGET THIS ONE. #BLESSED
[After the Tel Aviv concert.]

@ OHMYYYYY IM GETTING GOOSEBUMPS! @justinbieber
IS IN SINGAPORE!!" [Retweet from a fan.]

@ WHAT!?!? Singapore has heated toilet seats!?!
@kennyhamilton Score!! This really is a city from the future!
Lol.

@ Sydney goes hard!! Great show 2night… watched some of the royal wedding in the dressing room b4 the show. Looks like they needed a DJ. Lol. Congrats to William and Kate… and Kate's sister. She was a hit with @thattrygood.

MAY

The Show Must Go On

In May, Justin delighted fans and silenced critics by heading to Japan to play planned concerts in Osaka and Tokyo, despite radiation fears following a leak at a nuclear plant caused by the March earthquake and tsunami. JB showed himself to be mature and understanding of the plight of the Japanese people, leading by example when other artists were cancelling planned tours. Justin took to Twitter to announce he wasn't going to "be selfish" by staying away and also thanked his team for agreeing to accompany him on this last leg.

During his time in Japan, the star met with American ambassador John Roos and Canadian Ambassador Jonathan Fried. Afterwards Roos declared him, "A special young man sending out a message to the world," while Fried said, "You stand for the best of Canada."

Meeting Earthquake Victims

After the Osaka concert, Justin met with children from the town of Otsuchi – a place devastated by the tsunami. One boy read out a letter which said, 'We have friends who lost their family and their homes. The town is covered with wreckage and it will take a long time to get back to normal. But we will work hard for this. Please give us courage through your music.'

Justin was very moved and told the children, "Things can and will get better. There are only good times to come. My prayers are going to all of your families." In a final generous gesture Biebz, who had also contributed to the charity album 'Songs for Japan', announced via Twitter that he would donate a portion of the proceeds from his concerts to the Japanese Red Cross.

The Billboard Awards

The annual Billboard Awards are one of the most anticipated events in the music industry calendar. Biebz therefore was beside himself to learn that he was nominated in a massive 11 categories!

The star took his seat between Selena Gomez and his mum Pattie. Biebz himself was channelling Elvis Presley with his hair slicked up and a blinging gold tuxedo jacket by Canadian twin designers Dsquared2.

JB had the honour of presenting the award for Top Female Artist to pal Rihanna, who leapt on stage sporting a white suit and bobbed red hairdo. Rihanna proved herself to be another certified Belieber by saying, "Justin gave me my award… I'm so cool!" Biebz then sat back to enjoy the awesome show.

He said afterwards that he thought the performance of the night came from "My girl B – Queen B," aka Beyoncé, who was awarded The Billboard Milennium Award for her career achievements and was honoured by everyone from Michelle Obama to Stevie Wonder and Barbra Streisand.

He's A Winner!

Justin had to battle jetlag to attend the ceremony, but it was well worth it. He was stunned to win the Billboard.com Fan Favourite award – voted for by 6.5million people.

The star was then crowned Top New Artist, beating K$sha, Taio Cruz, Bruno Mars and Nicki Minaj to the award, which he accepted from Snoop Dog and techno poppers the Far East Movement. He thanked God who he said, "Has blessed me so much," before thanking his mum for putting up with him and of course his devoted Beliebers.

After that the awards kept coming. Host Eric Stonestreet – star of TV series Modern Family really had come as Elvis and he presented Justin with the award for Top Digital Media Artist.

Justin won seven trophies in all including Top Social Artist, Top Streaming Song for 'Baby', Top Streaming Artist and Top Pop Album for 'My World 2.0'. Backstage he couldn't stop smiling, telling his fans in an interview, "I want you to see how happy I am. You guys have made me into the person I am today."

40th Anniversary Of
The Hard Rock Café

Justin may have finished touring the world, but it turns out some of his belongings his haven't. May saw the launch of a touring exhibition of the world's largest collection of rock memorabilia. The tour, organized by Hard Rock International, featured 73,000 items donated by and belonging to some of the greatest names in the music industry – including Justin Drew Bieber.

Much of the collection is usually on display in the company's 171 restaurants, casinos and hotels, while the rest is warehoused, but to mark the 40th anniversary of the Hard Rock chain, the company decided to tour the memorabilia around the USA. The exhibition featured Jimi Hendrix's guitar, the wedding dress worn by Madonna in the 'Like A Virgin' music video, the red leather jacket seen on Michael Jackson in the 'Beat It' video, the dress Katy Perry wore for her 2008 Latin American awards when she leapt from the show's four-tier anniversary cake and JB's skateboard, seen in the music video for 'One Time.'

Acquiring such priceless items is a full-time job. Hard Rock employees follow bands and artists and buy memorabilia early on in their careers, betting on the artists' future potential – which has definitely paid off in Justin's case. Once the item is in the possession of the company it is in extremely good hands. John Galloway, chief marketing officer for Hard Rock explained, "If an artist gives us memorabilia, they assume we're going to take care of it and we're never going to sell it. We have a responsibility."

Tweets of the month

@ #HappyBDAYJAZZY – I want the whole world to know your big brother loves you!!!

@ Good day for fishing… I caught some small ones. :) @KennyHamilton is gonna cook em lol

@ Not gonna waste the opportunity. not gonna be selfish. not gonna get in my own way.
[When being advised not to go to Japan.]

@ Just met some incredible kids who have been thru alot because of the devastation here in Japan. blessed to meet them and proud to know them.

@ Dedicated #PRAY to the people of Japan tonight and the OLLG was one of the students i met yesterday. Really special night and a great show.

@ 10 Million and growing… and everyday I will make the effort to show appreciation. #neverchanging #ILOVEMYFANS.

@ For once waking up because of jet lag is great… because I just found out… we won 6 AWARDS 2nite! I THOUGHT IT WAS 3!!! CRAZY!! I have the GREATESTFANSINTHEWORLD !!! THANK U!!! I LOVE U I LOVE U I LOVE U!!

JUNE

The View TV Show

Biebz appeared on this popular panel show to talk about his perfume launch, looking cute and casual in a white tee, chinos and a blue cardigan.

Host Whoopi Goldberg asked Biebz to sing and he treated the mature audience – who were holding signs saying 'Seniors for Bieber' – to 'Never Say Never'. After discussing the fragrance, talk turned to the dangers of communicating via Twitter. Biebz said he needed to learn, "Not to tweet when I'm angry," but added that so far he had never accidentally tweeted something meant to be private – although his dad had once put his email address on a tweet which meant he was bombarded by emails from Beliebers.

Co-host Elisabeth Hasselbeck then challenged Biebz to a Segway race around set. JB easily won, riding the last few metres backwards. Biebz later pranked the panel, wandering into shot while they were trying to discuss a serious news story.

College Track

In June Biebz got behind another cause close to his heart – a charity called College Track that helps disadvantaged teenagers apply for university. Kind-hearted Justin agreed to perform free of charge in an intimate concert at the Mountain Winery venue in Saratoga, California. The proceeds of the ticket sales went to support the programme.

Justin's gesture won him two new celebrity fans. Hollywood star Ashton Kutcher, a supporter of College Track, tweeted, 'Hey @JustinBieber proud that you are playing a show for College Track. Good on you!' Rapper MC Hammer, who was also performing at the gig tweeted, 'Thanks for supporting College Track… You donated your time, talent and heart.'

Someday Fragrance Launch

With the launch of his perfume 'Someday', Justin became the first male celebrity to launch a fragrance for women.

Biebz and his team put a lot of thought into creating a product that would appeal to his fans. They worked with Swiss firm Firmenich, an international producer of perfumery, to develop a fruity blend, beautifully packaged in a bottle with a heart-shaped flower top and removable charms draped around the neck.

Justin personally approved the delicious scent and said, "Let's be real, the way a girl smells is very important to a guy! I have such a deep connection with my fans, so creating a fragrance that I personally love is another way I can bring them closer to my world."

The strapline for the ad campaign was *'Never let go'* and the commercial featured upcoming actress, Dree Hemingway spraying the scent on her neck and seeing Biebz appear before her eyes.

This is, of course, every fan's dream and Beliebers couldn't wait to get their hands on a bottle of the gorgeous scent. Within three weeks of launching in the US, sales had reached over $3million – making it the fastest-selling celebrity fragrance ever.

The launch of the perfume at mega-department store Macy's in New York's Herald Square was a huge deal with hundreds of fans queuing outside overnight for a glimpse of the star. Justin didn't want to disappoint them and after posing for pictures with his product headed outside for an impromptu meet-and-greet. Unfortunately however, the star had to be rushed back inside when an older man appeared to break out of the crowd and accost him. It was later reported that this was in fact an undercover policeman who was merely worried about Justin's safety as he approached the huge crowd.

The success of the perfume was very important to Justin as it was launched with one aim in mind – to raise money to help other people. Justin worked in partnership with a company called Give Back Brands to make sure that the net profits go to charities such as the Make A Wish Foundation and Pencils of Promise. "Not only am I able to create a fragrance for all my fans," he said, "but I'm also able to give back to charity, which is a huge priority for me. The people at Give Back Brands really get me and what I represent and care about."

JUNE

BET Awards

On 26th June, Biebz headed to the Shrine Auditorium in Los Angeles for the 2011 BET Awards, which, like the UK's MOBO Awards, celebrate talent from black and minority communities.

Biebz was rocking the distressed denim look with a 90s throwback acid-wash denim waistcoat paired with a black tee and metallic silver jeans. He accessorised big style with a skull necklace, tortoiseshell sunnies, a large watch, bracelets, a multi-coloured handkerchief in his top pocket and polka dot studded hi-tops. Only Jaden Smith – who wore orange, tiger-print denim jeans – could match him in the colour stakes on the red carpet.

Biebz was there, with Nicki Minaj, to co-present the award for Best Male Hip Hop Artist to pal Kanye West.

Playing Footy

Not every local football team can claim to have a global pop star as a player, but Stratford City FC can. Back home in Stratford, Ontario for a little downtime with family and friends, JB wasted no time in getting his local football club kit on.

He didn't have an amazing game, coming on in the second half, only to be sent off five minutes later with an injury, but his family and friends - including his dad and siblings Jazmyn and Jaxon, his grandparents and girlfriend Selena Gomez - were all there to lend support. While Selena and pals munched on fast food and giggled the game away, Biebz sat on the bench, chatting with team mates and cheering his team on to a 1–0 win. Go Stratford!

JUNE

MuchMusic Awards

On 19th June, Justin delighted fans by attending the annual MMVAs (MuchMusic Video Awards).

The star-studded bash, the biggest music awards ceremony in Canada, has been running since 1990. Biebz wasn't scheduled to perform or present on the night, although he was a nominee. So would he show? There was one big clue that he might attend – girlfriend Selena Gomez was co-hosting alongside film star Colin Farrell. So of course Justin loyally showed up on Selena's big night!

Biebz looked fab in a white suit jacket worn over retro t-shirt printed with a photo of Tiffani Amber Thiessen, star of 90s TV series *Saved By The Bell*. In a red carpet interview before the show, he revealed he was in talks with Mark Wahlberg about a new film project, which would give him a chance to show off his "athleticism". He also said the performance he was most looking forward to seeing was Selena singing her hit song *'Who Says'*.

Selena dazzled in several outfits and looked delighted when she announced JB had won Best International Video of the Year for *'Somebody to Love feat. Usher'*, tying with rapper Drake, for the award. JB bounded onstage and shook Selena's hand, joking "Selena, nice to meet you I'm Justin. You're very beautiful… maybe we could go out some time." The pair really had a night to remember; Selena smashed it on stage and Justin went on to scoop the UR Fave Artist Award for *'Somebody to Love'*. Yay!

MTV Movie and CMT Awards

It was a month of plenty for Biebz, as the award shows — and statuettes - kept rolling in.

He dropped in unexpectedly at the 2011 MTV Movie Awards to claim his Golden Popcorn award in the Best Jaw Dropping Moment category for *Never Say Never*. Then, just three days later, he attended the CMT Awards in Nashville, Tennessee. The awards, which honour the best country music videos of the year, seemed an unlikely hangout for a prince of pop like Biebz… Except, JB's clever decision to team up with country group Rascal Flatts on *'That Should Be Me'* won them the Collaborative Video of the Year Award. "It was an honour to appear in the video with you. We got Bieber Fever!" said lead singer Gary LeVox.

B-Ball and Birthday Bash

Biebz had just one thing on his mind on the 8th and 9th of June - basketball. The star headed to The American Airlines Center in Dallas, to watch games four and five of the NBA finals between the home team, the Dallas Mavericks and the Miami Heat. On the 8th, the star shared his luxury box with girlfriend Selena, and the superstar couple tried their best to concentrate on the game and not each other!

The following day, the 9th, Justin mingled with the crowd and met NBA legend Sam Perkins in the dressing rooms. Despite the fact that JB showed his support to the Heat, even sporting a T-shirt in their colours, the Mavs ended up taking the series by winning four games to Miami's two.

On the 18th, Justin had an appointment which was not to be missed. It was his manager Scooter Braun's 30th birthday and Usher, Biebz and pals threw a party to remember for the man who discovered Biebz, at The Music Box Theatre in Hollywood.

Usher served as MC along with Scooter's brother Adam. Biebz hung out with pal Jaden Smith and later performed 'Never Say Never' and 'Baby' with him. Usher, Maroon 5 frontman Adam Levine and MC Hammer also hit the stage in tribute to Scooter. The entertainment included fire throwers, belly dancers and the guest list was a cast of LA lovelies including Kim Kardashian and Paris Hilton. Wild!

Tweets of the month

@ Tonight we are all just happy. Great night. We did that show for all the right reasons. 2nite my fans helped #makeachange with College Track. Also thanks to the fans for helping me take a moment for @seankingston b4 eenie meenie 2nite. Get better big bro. We miss u

@ Having a great time at the #betawards. Getting ready to get on stage with my girl @nickiminaj

@ The ladies of @theviewtv thank you for having me. awesome as always…sorry for the prank. lol. #someday and @ehasselbeck good try good try. lol. #segwayswag

@ @brunomars you def killed it and @selenagomez you did a great job and were lookin good. nice meeting you. lol. ;)

@ Gonna chill..grab a bite..then see everyone at MACY's for the #SOMEDAY launch. LEGGO!!

@ The big day is here. You are an old man now @scooterbraun. Lol. With love #HAPPYBIRTHDAYSCOOTER.

ESPY Awards

The Espys are the only sports show on the American awards schedule – they're the equivalent of the Sports Personality of the Year awards in the UK. So sports-mad Biebz was of course only too happy to present the final award of the evening, the award for Best Team, to NBA champions the Dallas Mavericks. He took to the stage wearing a blue NASCAR racing jumpsuit in honour of his co-presenter, indie racing driver Danika Patrick.

Biebz wasn't the only famous Justin presenting an award that night, almost-mentor Justin Timberlake was there too! It turned out that Biebz had another celebrity fan, as Olympic alpine skier Lindsey Vonn declared her Bieber fever when she won the award for Best Female Athlete, for the second year running, and gushed in her acceptance speech, "Justin Bieber. Will you take a picture with me afterwards, for my Facebook page?" JB, who was sitting with Selena – in a jersey sheer inset jumper by Christian Cota - laughed and nodded and, after the show, Lindsey hopped on Twitter and proudly posted her pic saying: 'I finally got my Justin Bieber pic! LV #bieberfever #espys'. She also received over a thousand likes after posting it on her Facebook page too!

AUGUST

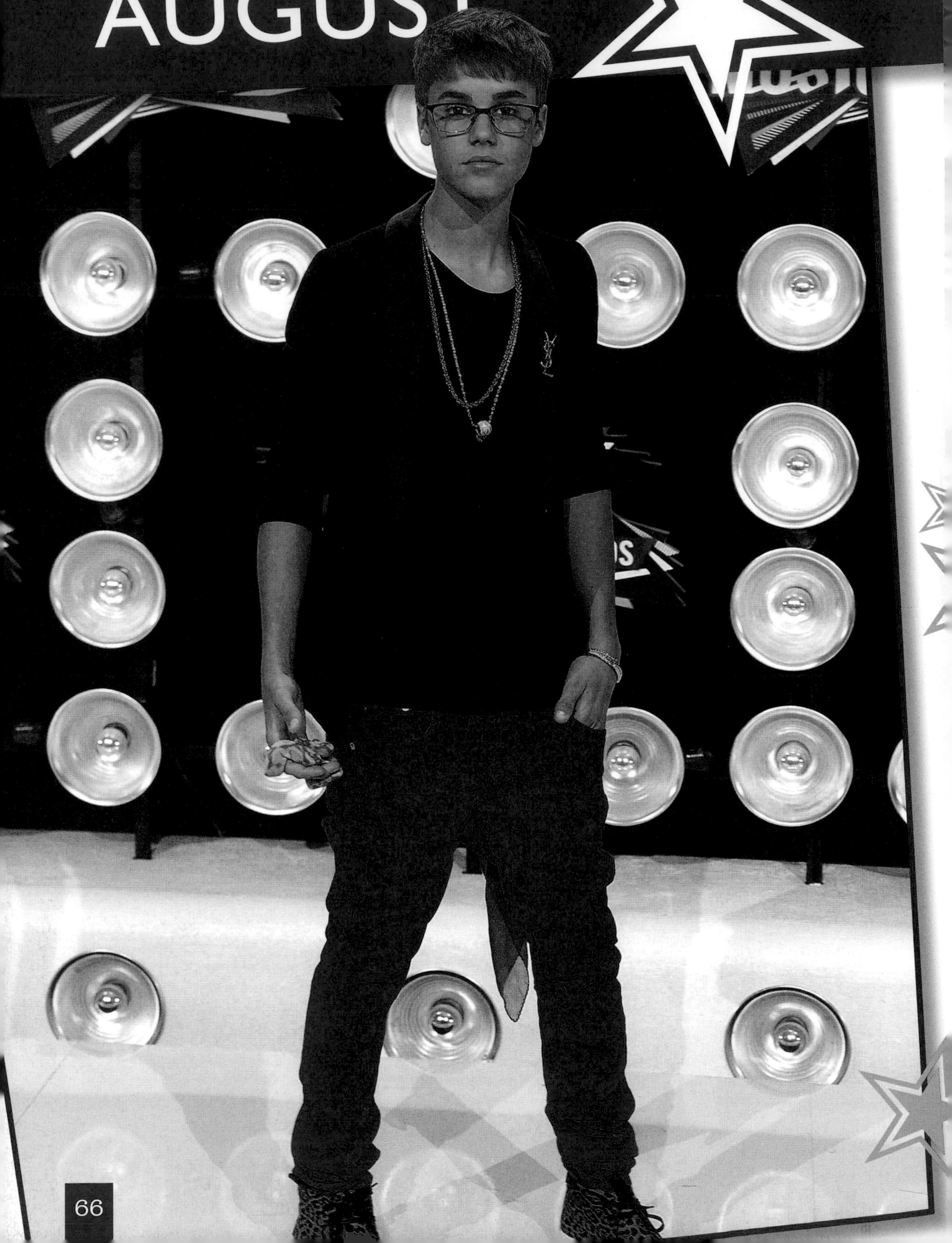

MTV Video Music Awards

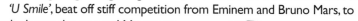

Biebz caused minor hiss-teria among the waiting press, when he turned up on the red carpet at the MTV Video Music Awards with a new squeeze - a baby constrictor called Johnson – apparently his new pet. The tiny snake, with striking yellow-markings, spent the evening wrapped tightly round Justin's fingers like a knuckleduster – in fact Justin even mentioned it as if it was part of his outfit. Selena Gomez was conducting pre-show interviews for MTV and pulling him aside for an interview asked, "Who are you wearing? Can you please talk to me about that?" Biebz replied, "I have my snake, I have red pants and I have cheetah shoes!" before planting a big kiss on her cheek. The amphibian guest proved a talking point that night, with stars such as actor Paul Rudd stopping to stroke it and interviewers fleeing at the sight of it. In reply to a journalist who asked "A snake? Why?" JB replied, "Why not?" He also confided. "It'll get like, four feet long. It's gonna get big!" Biebz, nominated for Best Male Video, for 'U Smile', beat off stiff competition from Eminem and Bruno Mars, to take home the coveted Moonman.

Teen Choice Awards

Bieber haters may have thought they had something to celebrate in July when the object of their resentment was crowned Choice Twit at the Teen Choice Awards. Unfortunately for them, this was an honour, as it meant voters were in fact rewarding Biebz for having posted the best tweet of the year on Twitter. After that it got worse – for the haters that is – as Justin scooped three more Surfboard awards for Choice Male Artist, Choice TV Villain (for his role in *C.S.I.*) and Choice Male Hottie. And, if that seemed like a good night's work, girlfriend Selena Gomez had an even bigger haul of silverware, taking home a whopping five awards and pipping JB to the title of biggest winner of the night. Selena won Choice TV Actress (in a comedy), Choice Female Hottie, Choice Music Group (Selena Gomez & The Scene), Choice Music Single (for '*Who Says*') and Choice Love Song (for '*Love You Like a Love Song*').

The superstar couple arrived separately at the venue – the Gibson Amphitheatre in Universal City, California. Selena had flown in from New York by private jet the night before and spent the day rehearsing for her big performance with her musicians and a pair of tango dancers. Selena filmed a mini-clip of the run-up to the award show, which she posted online. It showed her running through vocal warm-up exercises in her dressing room with JB and allowing him into her pre-show ritual group prayer, where she asked that she could bring smiles to people's faces. When the evening ceremony began, Biebz worked the blue carpet alone, while Selena posed for photos with her BFF and fellow Disney-ite Demi Lovato. All three looked fresh and summery. Demi – who took home the Choice Inspire award and the Choice Song of the Summer (for '*Skyscraper*') - wore a yellow BCBGMaxAzria dress with Louboutin platforms, while Selena shimmered in a gold Erin Fetherston gown. Not to be outdone in the fashion-stakes, Biebz wore a dusty-rose tailored shirt and matching flower buttonhole, topped with an edgy biker vest, bowtie, black jeans and hi-tops. Once inside, Selena changed into a metallic silver and nude lace dress by British designer Julien MacDonald, teamed with strappy heels. She and Biebz sat next to each other and happily posed for photographs. Selena performed '*Love You Like A Love Song*' with her band The Scene and Biebz was on his feet,

JUSTIN BIEBER

dancing away and mouthing the lyrics
Sweet! Then it was Justin's turn on stage to accept
Choice Male Hottie, "Three years ago, I was chilling on a couch
in Canada watching the Teen Choice Awards, and now I'm here," he said, in his
acceptance speech. "Anything is possible if you set your mind to it."

AUGUST

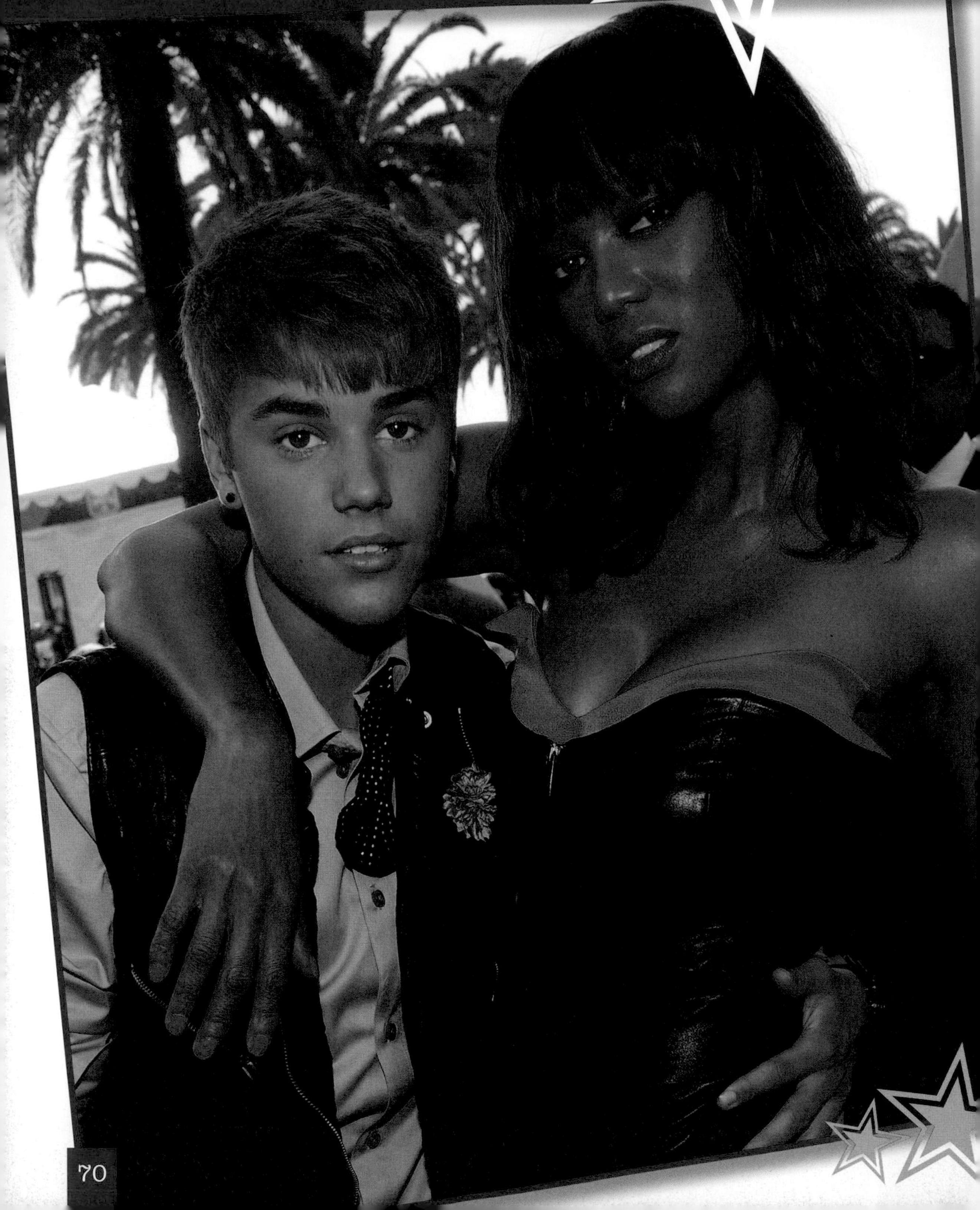

Teen Choice Awards

Although Biebz loves to win awards, he always says that he's there first and foremost "to have fun." The Teen Choice awards were no exception, providing the ideal opportunity for JB to kick back with some of his celeb buddies. A long time friend of Taylor Swift – having opened for her on tour in London – the pair sat together in the auditorium, chatting and catching up. Best buddy and 'Eenie Meenie' collaborator Sean Kingston was also there and presented Biebz with one of his four awards. The pair, who hit it off while working together, became really tight after Sean was nearly killed in a jet-ski accident in May. Seeing his friend on stage, fighting fit and healthy again must have been just as special for JB as getting the award itself. Tyra Banks also presented Justin with one of his awards and Biebz posed with the statuesque supermodel and TV presenter on the blue carpet.

AUGUST

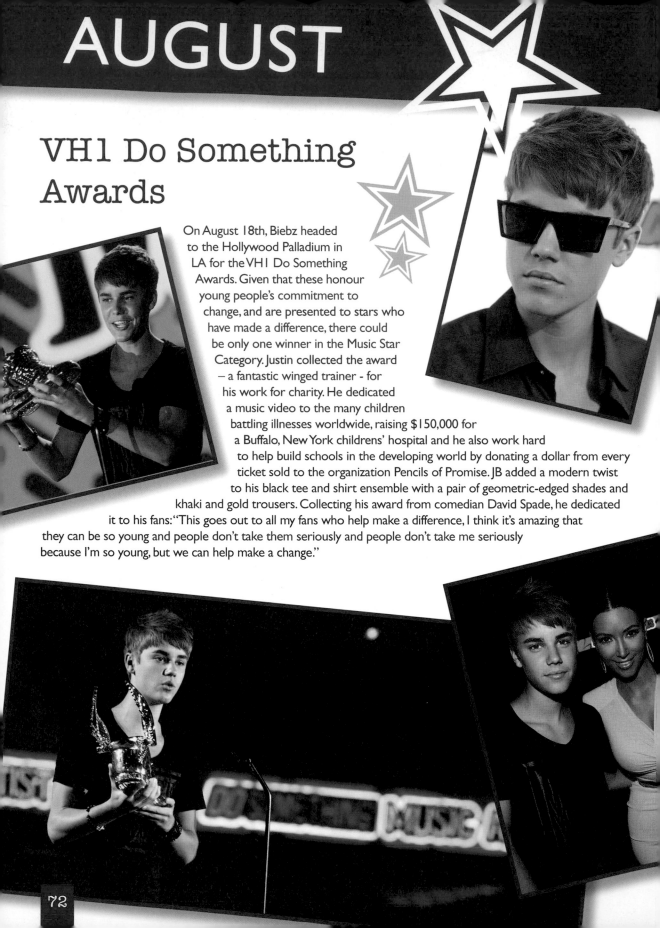

VH1 Do Something Awards

On August 18th, Biebz headed to the Hollywood Palladium in LA for the VH1 Do Something Awards. Given that these honour young people's commitment to change, and are presented to stars who have made a difference, there could be only one winner in the Music Star Category. Justin collected the award – a fantastic winged trainer - for his work for charity. He dedicated a music video to the many children battling illnesses worldwide, raising $150,000 for a Buffalo, New York childrens' hospital and he also work hard to help build schools in the developing world by donating a dollar from every ticket sold to the organization Pencils of Promise. JB added a modern twist to his black tee and shirt ensemble with a pair of geometric-edged shades and khaki and gold trousers. Collecting his award from comedian David Spade, he dedicated it to his fans: "This goes out to all my fans who help make a difference, I think it's amazing that they can be so young and people don't take them seriously and people don't take me seriously because I'm so young, but we can help make a change."

Tweets of the month

@ Gotta say thank u and congrats to my dude @ColinTilley for his first #VMA win for U SMILE!! he was the director and he is a #beast.'

@ @Taylorswift13 has been there from day 1. true friend. #goodtimes

@ Will and Jada are one of the best couples ever. #FACT #real.

@ HumanitarianDay" #HappyWorldHumanitarianDay to all the causes out there like @pencilsofpromis and @Medishare4Haiti working to #makeachange!

@ In the studio writing with @TrickyStewart - last time this happened a song called BABY happened. LEGGO. #believe.

@ MEXICO!! got news that the stadium in Monterrey is already SOLD OUT!! 2 Hours!! Gracias!!! MEXICO CITY IS NEXT!! LEGGO!! TE AMO MUCHO.

Fashion's Night Out

Biebz and his manager Scooter, mentor Usher and mum Pattie, all attended the annual Fashion's Night Out event at Manhattan's Dolce and Gabbana store on the 8th September. Arriving at the boutique located on Madison Avenue and 69th Street, Biebz waved to fans and posed for photographers. He was, of course, dressed head to toe in pieces from his favourite designers' latest collection - including an awesome purple leather jacket and grey stonewashed jeans. Glee's Lea Michele was also there, along with American Vogue magazine editor Anna Wintour. Wintour is the brains behind Fashion's Night Out which has gone on to become a global shopping bonanza with shoppers converging on retailers in cities around the world to party and spend at the same time.

Biebz was at the event to sign items for his fans and the hundreds of Beliebers who showed up bought everything from small items of make-up to D&G T-shirts costing nearly $200. Proceeds from the event went to charity Pencils of Promise which helps fund education in third world countries. It's a charity very close to Justin's heart and the hard-working and generous lad did his bit by signing his autograph for two hours. Biebz had also hoped to walk around and meet and greet fans, but the store was so overcrowded there were health and safety fears and he had to remain upstairs for most of the night. Still, never one to let protocol come between him and his faithful Beliebers, Biebz eventually appeared on the stairs where he

danced around with Usher, Scooter and rapper Asher Roth. Then, he gave a brilliant, surprise performance of Asher's song 'I Love College'.

It was a night where the city that never sleeps, really didn't get much shuteye. There were parties uptown, downtown and all around Manhattan. Canadian rapper Drake was DJing at Versace, Nicki Minaj appeared at shoe designer Guiseppe Zanotti's boutique, Joe Jonas was on stage at Sak's department store and Joss Stone sang at Macy's.

Over in the Meat Packing District, former High School Musical star Vanessa Hudgens spun the decks at Pop Chips Playland and Estelle played a gig at Diane Von Furstenberg's boutique.

SEPTEMBER

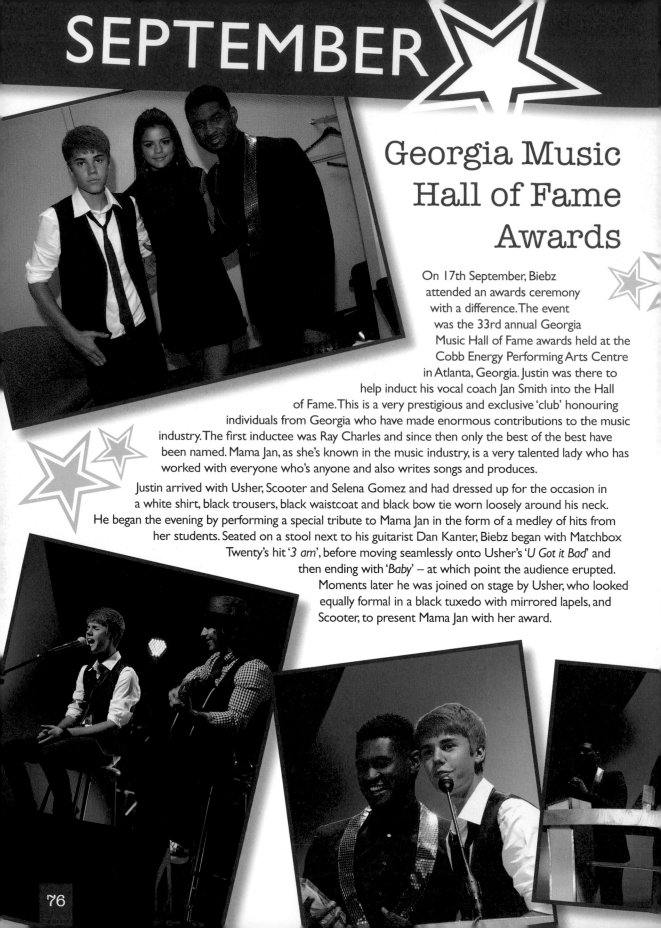

Georgia Music Hall of Fame Awards

On 17th September, Biebz attended an awards ceremony with a difference. The event was the 33rd annual Georgia Music Hall of Fame awards held at the Cobb Energy Performing Arts Centre in Atlanta, Georgia. Justin was there to help induct his vocal coach Jan Smith into the Hall of Fame. This is a very prestigious and exclusive 'club' honouring individuals from Georgia who have made enormous contributions to the music industry. The first inductee was Ray Charles and since then only the best of the best have been named. Mama Jan, as she's known in the music industry, is a very talented lady who has worked with everyone who's anyone and also writes songs and produces.

Justin arrived with Usher, Scooter and Selena Gomez and had dressed up for the occasion in a white shirt, black trousers, black waistcoat and black bow tie worn loosely around his neck. He began the evening by performing a special tribute to Mama Jan in the form of a medley of hits from her students. Seated on a stool next to his guitarist Dan Kanter, Biebz began with Matchbox Twenty's hit '3 am', before moving seamlessly onto Usher's 'U Got it Bad' and then ending with 'Baby' – at which point the audience erupted. Moments later he was joined on stage by Usher, who looked equally formal in a black tuxedo with mirrored lapels, and Scooter, to present Mama Jan with her award.

Passing her the trophy, Justin smothered Mama Jan with kisses, and then pumped his fist in the air to get the audience cheering. Usher too, showed how fond he is of his voice coach. He gave her a great big hug and then made a speech where he called her "a treasure to Atlanta," telling the crowd about how she had helped him regain his voice after he'd thought his career was over for good.

In her acceptance speech, Mama Jan seemed overcome. She said, "I'm very humbled by all of the artists who lend their celebrity to me and I'm proud to be part of their success." Later in the show, Smith returned the favour by presenting Justin with the Horizon Award, which, although not an induction into the celebrated Hall of Fame, recognises young performers for their outstanding achievements. As Justin came up on stage Jan showed just how close they'd become by saying, "One of the greatest things about Jellybean, is that his heart is still the same. He's the same little guy I met in December 2008," Upon taking his award, Bieber said that since he moved to Atlanta as soon as he got his record deal, "I developed a nice family and friends. I would consider Atlanta my second home."

LudaDay in Atlanta

Biebz is usually so polite and well mannered. But he was talking kinda trashy on Twitter in the run up to a charity basketball game in Atlanta on September 4th. He tweeted six times in a row about the LudaDay Weekend Celeb Basketball Game talking himself up and throwing down the gauntlet to rapper Ludacris. One tweet said "@Ludacris u are a good man… but #teambieber is gonna kill u on Sunday." LudaDay Weekend has become legendary in Atlanta. The brainchild of Ludacris (real name Chris Bridges), it is a series of events and parties held over Labour Day weekend each year in Atlanta, with the aim of giving back to the community and raising money for charity. The sporting highlight of the weekend is the celebrity basketball game and for this, the sixth year of the event, Ludacris had assembled two awesome teams of including NBA stars Kevin Durant, Carmelo Anthony and Chris Paul, to play under the banners of Team Ludacris and Team Bieber. In the run up to the event Luda, who worked with Biebz on 'Baby' and jokingly calls him 'his mentor' said he was definitely not going to let Justin win the game. However, things don't always work out as we hope and on the day the Canadian crooner and his team beat Luda's lot by two points, with the final score 134-132. Still, Ludacris owed himself a big pat on the back as this event alone raised $10,000 for charity.

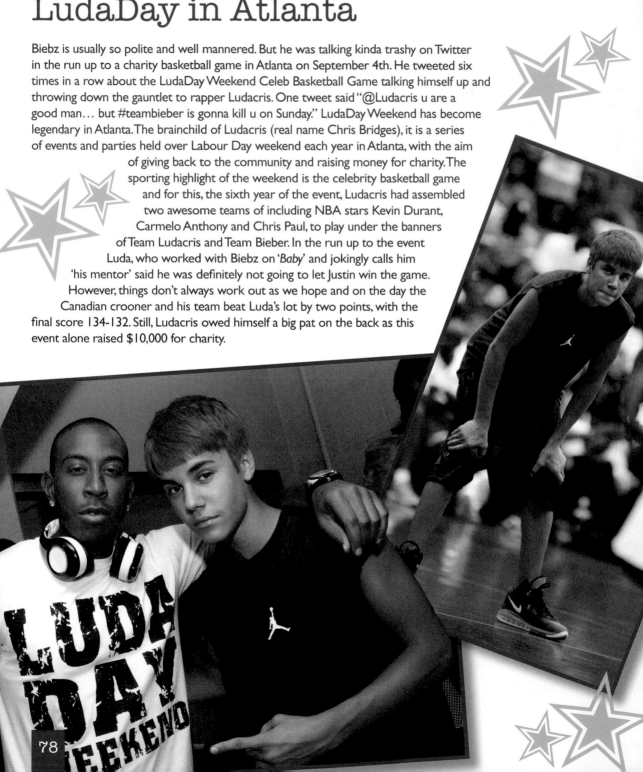

OCTOBER

TOUR DATES: SOUTH AMERICA

Oct 5	Rio di Janeiro	BRAZIL	Brazil Engenhao
Oct 8	Sao Paulo	BRAZIL	Morumbi Stadium
Oct 10	Rio Grande	BRAZIL	Estadio Jose Pinheiro Borda
Oct 12	Buenos Aires	ARGENTINA	River Plate Stadium
Oct 13	Buenos Aires	ARGENTINA	River Plate Stadium
Oct 15	Santiago	CHILE	Estadio Julio Martinez Pradanos
Oct 19	Caracas	VENEZUELA	Simon Bolivar University

OCTOBER

Brazil, Argentina, Chile and Venezuela

It's hot in South America, and perhaps that explains why Bieber Fever raged out of control at times during the last leg of his tour. Justin took Selena along for the Brazil dates and brought her out on stage as a special guest to perform 'Who Says' in Rio. He left the stage, but returned to duet with her for the end and afterwards the two shared a sizzling embrace. Justin and Selena stayed at the Copacabana Palace overlooking the famous beach in Rio. They enjoyed butler service and their swanky suite even had a private swimming pool with a bar sunk in it, meaning they could sip refreshing drinks while they swam. Smokin' hot British boy-band The Wanted opened for Justin in Sao Paolo, Brazil, turning the heat up another notch.

But things really got crazy when Biebz flew in to play dates in Argentina. In Buenos Aires, a group of crazy Beliebers tried to smash their way into Justin's hotel moments after he appeared on the balcony to greet fans. Police had to respond pretty quickly to remove the determined girls. Fortunately Biebz saw the funny side. "My fans go HARD!!" he tweeted on 12th October. "Wait, but don't break into my room. That ain't cool. But this is still epic!"

Unfortunately it was a similar story in Chile where a mob of hundreds of fans went loco outside his hotel – the W – in Santiago. Luckily Biebz hadn't yet left Buenos Aires. But the Chilean authorities were so worried about the out of control crowd they contacted Justin's camp and requested he arrive at the hotel by helicopter rather than by car, to keep fans from swarming in and mobbing him! Crazy Times!

But, despite the general Bieber-led insanity the show went well. He danced his way through '*Bigger*', vamped for the crowd during '*U Smile*' and slowed things down for an acoustic set, serenading the girls and making his signature two-handed heart gesture, causing every heart in the stadium to skip a beat.

When Biebz finally flew in to Caracas, Venezuela he had to be kept from throngs of girls who had been camping out for 14 hours to see him, again due to security issues. Instead, Biebz went straight off to prepare for the concert, which was to be very special as it was the last in a tour that had taken him to five continents over almost two years. Although Biebz had admitted he'd be glad to put the *My World* set list to bed, he was elated to have brought so much joy to so many people and celebrated the occasion in style by jumping out onstage at the end of the concert shirtless, showing his buff torso.

Happy Halloween with Jay Leno

A figure, clad head to toe in black, suddenly appeared in a Manhattan TV studio on Halloween. Spooky? Nah! Actually, it was just Biebz in a wet-look black shirt, tie and jeans, popping in for a chat with Jay Leno. Biebz talked about everything from his favourite trick-or-treating costume as a kid – a construction worker, with overalls and a hardhat borrowed from his dad and a moustache drawn on in black pen, to his perfume.

He also talked about his best ever Christmas present – a red two-wheeler bike that he couldn't ride for months, because there was too much snow. Now of course, he's all about cars – and he and Jay discussed his latest – a flat matt black Cadillac customised to look like the bat mobile. The naughty boy admitted he'd already got one ticket for speeding.

Then he gave viewers the heads-up about his Christmas album 'Mistletoe' which features him duetting with big names like Mariah Carey. Biebz admitted Mariah's famous vocal range in 'All I Want For Christmas' caused him a few problems. "She has super high notes and it's not like she was going to change the key for me, so I had to go in and do it in her key."

Finally Biebz topped off a great interview by telling Jay that the city he most enjoyed visiting during his world tour was Tokyo and that sushi is "his favourite", bringing on a plate of the raw fish delicacies for Jay Leno to try.

Ice Ice Bieber

We all know how much Biebz loves ice hockey and just because he's often based in LA it doesn't mean he has to miss out. Biebz and pal Sean Kingston were spotted catching the Los Angeles Kings play the New Jersey Devils at the Staples Centre on 25th of the month. Although he's a die-hard Toronto Maple Leafs fan, Biebz seems to have adopted the LA Kings as his favourite US side, as he sported their baseball cap. On this occasion however, he went home disappointed, as his team and lost 0-3. JB also wore several silicone Love for Lokomotiv Memory Bracelets on one wrist. The wives and girlfriends of Kings players had been selling them to raise money for the families and children of the Russian ice-hockey team Lokomotiv Yaroslavl, all but two of whom were killed in a plane crash on 7th September 2011.

A Bad Waxing Job

This month Biebz got waxed again. No, not his chest or his eyebrows! His entire self was immortalised for another famous wax museum – the Madrid Wax Museum, in Spain. Biebz may be very special, but even he can't be in two places at one time, so, as Justin's hectic work schedule had him in the States, he was unable to attend the official unveiling, which, it turned out may have been a blessing for all concerned. The clothes, a grey 'King's Rowe' hoody over a purple tee, baggy jeans and hi-tops, were spot on, but as for the rest... Urgh!

The skin looked baggy, the hair-do, out-dated and the eyes, wrong. While on the couch, appearing on the *Late Show with David Letterman*, Biebz was shown photos of the figure, which he branded "awful!" "It doesn't look like me at all," he added, and when told that the figure was on display at the Madrid Wax Museum said grimly "I don't know what they were thinking." Celeb-watcher Perez Hilton got online to brand it "the most horrifying wax figurine ever" and Beliebers seemed to be in total agreement, with fans around the world taking to online chat rooms and forums to express their misgivings. Comments ranged from "Jeez, his eyes are totally wrong, there is no sparkle, no life…" to "Why does it look all creepy like that? Somebody needs to fix this now!" and "The wax looks sooooo much older than the real Justin. Poor JB, if he has to go there and say 'thanks' for it!" Biebz must have been thinking exactly the same thing.

Tweets of the month

@ Had a lil fun last night in RIO ... show #2 in RIO is 2nite ... got some very special guests with me 2nite. #Mistletoe.

@ Played the album #UnderTheMistletoe for my big bros Pharrell and @UsherRaymondIV - less than #24Hours to go.. WE READY!!

@ #hockey is a real man's sport. #proudCanadian.

@ What a great dinner I just had! thanks to @seankingston mom @mamakingston who just throw down some great Jamaican style steak haha.

@ Hey @westfieldlondon & @westfieldstrat gonna see u on the 7th November! UK, who's coming?! #westfieldbieber.

@ Did 4 hours of international press yesterday...woke up at 5:30 this morning to do radio phoners and now off to do interviews. yep... #5DAYS!

Westfield Christmas Lights

Tis the season to Bieb jolly! As the nights drew in and the temperature dropped, we Brits at least had something to look forward to other than an annual visit from Santa. Biebz was in town and he had something particularly special to do! Justin got to switch the Christmas lights on at not one, but both the incredibly hip new Westfield shopping centres, or 'malls' as he would probably call them.

Biebz began his marathon day at the site in Shepherd's Bush, West London where, after welcoming members of the Teenage Cancer Trust charity onstage to witness him switching on the lights, he performed tracks from his new album 'Underneath The Mistletoe'. The delighted audience included former Spice Girl Geri Halliwell, and Biebz was joined on stage by The Wanted who admitted they were just there 'gate-crashing Bieber's lights party'. The boys had a backslapping fest to the sounds of The Wanted's 'Lightning', waved at the crowd and then left JB to finish the concert.

Then it was on to Stratford, East London. The star was flown by helicopter to Stratford, East London. Hundreds more fans had queued overnight there to get a coveted wristband which would permit them entrance to the venue, even travelling from places like Norway, to catch a glimpse of JB. Introduced by Radio 1 DJ Reggie Yates, Biebz bounded onstage in a Grey beanie, black baseball jacket, black tee and jeans to play the same set, whipping everyone up into a frenzy by announcing, "My favourite thing about London is the girls!" The charmer!

'Under The Mistletoe' Release

Lovely Justin wanted to give his fans a Christmas treat in their stockings or under the tree – in the shape of his album of Christmas songs. 'Under The Mistletoe' was released on 1st November and featured a mix of funky versions of classic songs and new tracks including 'Mistletoe', which was pre-released at the end of October as a taster of what was to come.

The music video for 'Mistletoe' feature JB in a snowy town, romancing a lucky girl (real name Allie Williams, a model based in Tennessee), shopping for gifts, taking photo-booth snapshots and even snogging her under the mistletoe! Biebz, who worked with a host of talent to create the disc told chat show host Ellen "It's completely different, it's like my best album so far". Which can't have hindered sales as the album shifted over 200,000 copies in a week, shooting it to number one on The billboard 100 in the States.

This meant Biebz broke two records, becoming the first star under the age of 18 ever to have three number one albums, and also to become the first male star to have a number one with a Christmas album.

There were 11 tracks in all, with 15 on the deluxe version plus 25 minutes of unseen Bieber footage. As usual, Biebz proved to be a clever collaborator, working with rapper Busta Rhymes on 'The Drummer Boy', Usher on 'The Christmas Song' and Boyz II Men on 'Fa La La'. The track 'Santa Claus is Coming to Town' was featured in the opening credits of the hit movie Arthur Christmas and the video for the track was shown exclusively as a trailer in cinemas. Biebz cannily released some behind-the-scenes footage showing him shooting the clip, with a Santa's' workshop set, toys that come to life and dance, and JB drumming his heart out.

But perhaps the piece-de-resistance of the whole album came with his duet with Mariah Carey. Filmed in Macy's department store it showed Mariah in a Christmas outfit and in a sleigh handing out gifts with Biebz.

The album was unique too for the fact that Universal, the record label, agreed that a portion of profits from sales could go to Justin's Believe charity drive. This helps a number of charities including one – The House of Blessing Food bank in Ontario, a charity particularly close to JB's heart. Biebz revealed in interviews that his mum used to go there to get food for them at Christmas, back in the days when they had very little. "Mum went to the food bank so it's great to be able to give back," he said.

"I didn't know I was less fortunate, she was really good at hiding it, she always made sure I was taken care of, so if I'm able to give back now, then that's the greatest Christmas gift of all."

While promoting the album Biebz talked a lot about the importance of spending Christmas with his family, parents, grandparents, brother and sister and also about traditions, such as his stocking – revealing that mum, Pattie usually buys long, skinny ones and fills them with necessities like toothbrushes, toothpaste and sweets – just as she has all his life. JB also revealed he loves Christmas songs in general, the cornier the better with his fave being 'Rudolf the Red-nosed Reindeer'. Awww!

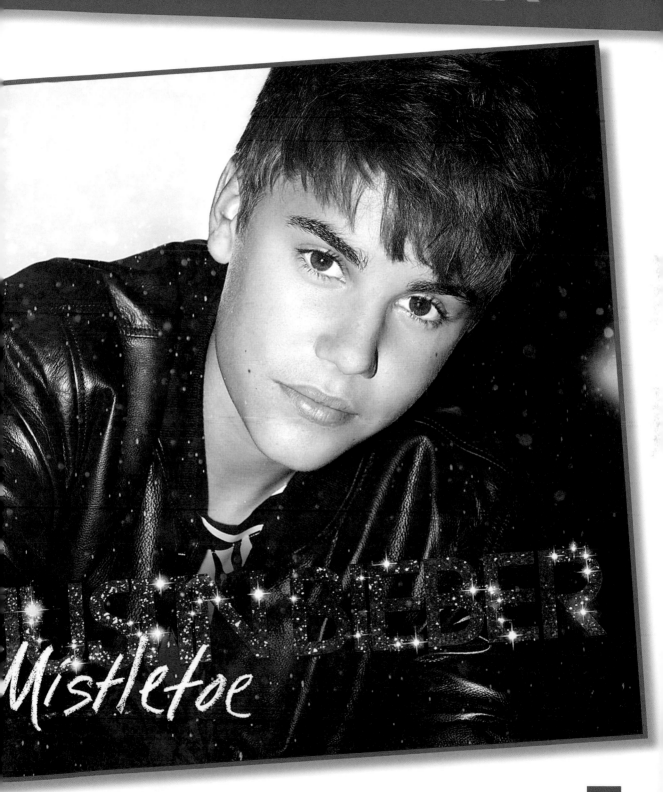

American Music Awards

Biebz and Selena stole the show at the American Music Awards in LA. Turning up in a white vintage Packard Super 8 car, they both looked as if they had just walked off the set of Bugsy Malone. JB wore a black tux with white shirt and black bow tie and wore his hair in a slicked back matinee idol style. While Selena looked equally glamorous in a backless champagne coloured satin gown by Giorgio Armani with a dropped waist and classy, loosely-curled locks. JB missed out on Best Male Artist to Bruno Mars, but went on to light up the stage,

Performing with LMFAO

Biebz began by performing '*Mistletoe*' in red and white leather trousers and jacket, but it was his end of the night slot with LMFAO that really got the par-tay started. The rappers launched into their '*Party Rock Anthem*' and then suddenly – there was Biebz, resplendent in a pair of yellow tiger-striped Zubaz trousers, a trademark LMFAO item, and a black cut-off tee. JB joined the boys for a spot of shuffling and really gave it some welly! In the audience Katy Perry and Selena Gomez boogied away clad in 3D glasses shaking inflatable clap sticks. Meanwhile on stage, Redfoo and Sky Blu cheered Justin on, yelling "Yo Bieber, Yo Bieber!" Classic!

NOVEMBER

On the Pitch at Chelsea FC

While in London, Biebz just couldn't wait to visit one of the city's biggest clubs, Chelsea FC. The star, accompanied by DJ and presenter Reggie Yates, and also reportedly by Selena Gomez – headed to Stamford Bridge on the Fulham Road in Chelsea and was given a full, guided tour of the amazing stadium before being presented with a Blues kit. Biebz wasted no time donning it and heading on to the sacred turf for a kick-about with some of the club's leading lights including Frank Lampard and Fernando Torres. Biebz showed once again that he's none too shoddy with a ball at his feet, outshining Torres with some ball control skills – rather embarrassingly given that the visit was being filmed by ITV for a forthcoming show *This is Justin Bieber*. The trio then headed off to look at the dressing rooms where Biebz' hit 'Baby' was playing over the speakers. Who knew that this is how the Blues chillax!

European MTV Awards

Biebz and Gaga reigned supreme at the European MTV awards held in Belfast, Northern Ireland. While Gaga scooped Best Female, Best Song and Best Video for '*Born This Way*', Biebz was crowned Best Male, beating Eminem and Kanye West. As he came off stage, Ludacris caught up with him and presented him with the award for Best Pop Act too. Biebz was also honoured by the music TV station with the MTV Voices award for his charity work and attended a special dinner in his honour on the eve of the show. On the night, Justin looked casual in an open-necked lumber shirt under a charcoal grey crew-neck sweater. He later changed into a black leather jacket and trousers, featuring a motif by the late pop artist Keith Haring before performing a mix of '*Mistletoe*' and '*Never Say Never*'. Meanwhile, girlfriend Selena Gomez was showing her professional credentials by hosting the entire show in a stream of ever more gorgeous dresses.

On the Air

In the US again, JB paid a morning visit to Z100 Radio Station in New York City. The star kept warm with a navy and yellow winter bobble hat. The DJ quizzed him about accusations that he'd fathered a baby. Biebz said, "As far as the whole, you know, baby situation, you know, it's unfortunate that it had to happen like that, that you know people make false accusations, but things happen in this industry and you just have to keep your head high and be positive, and that's really all I have to say."

German X-Factor

Continuing the European promotion of 'Under The Mistletoe', Biebz turned up on the German version of the X Factor. He performed 'Mistletoe' in a military-style red sleeveless jacket over a black sweater with black gloves. Biebz serenaded judge Sarah Connor and told the contestants the good and bad things about being a pop star. "You get to travel the world and see so many places. But it's hard being away from my family and also there are a lot of bad rumours so you have to be a strong person".

Tweets of the month

@ I'M SEXY AND I KNOW IT!

@ I hear melodies when your heart beats.

@ Just received my first EMA this year...got the award for our charity work. I say OUR because we do it together....

@ So I think everyone needs to go see my new music vid for "Santa Claus Is Comin To Town" in theatres TODAY on the new movie #ArthurChristmas.

@ HAPPY BIRTHDAY JAXO!! YOUR BIG BROTHER LOVES YOU!! #HappyBirthdayJaxon.

@ Shoutout to my big sis and DEF JAM labelmate @ rihanna for her new album OUT NOW!! GET THAT!

@ Thanks to everyone out there doing BUYOUTS for #UnderTheMistletoe album. Incredible to see u all come together. Thank u!

DECEMBER

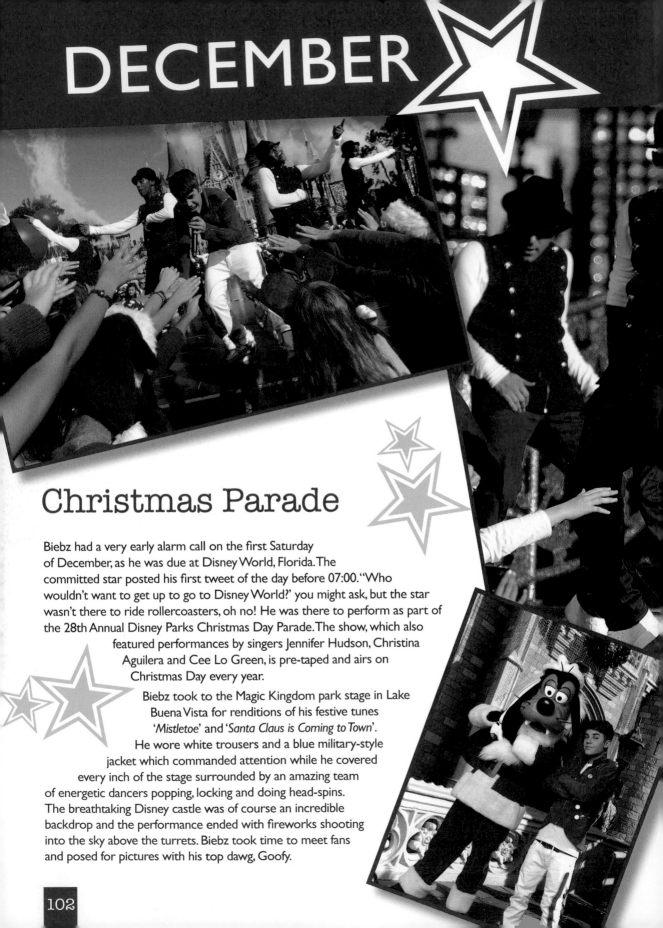

Christmas Parade

Biebz had a very early alarm call on the first Saturday of December, as he was due at Disney World, Florida. The committed star posted his first tweet of the day before 07:00. "Who wouldn't want to get up to go to Disney World?" you might ask, but the star wasn't there to ride rollercoasters, oh no! He was there to perform as part of the 28th Annual Disney Parks Christmas Day Parade. The show, which also featured performances by singers Jennifer Hudson, Christina Aguilera and Cee Lo Green, is pre-taped and airs on Christmas Day every year.

Biebz took to the Magic Kingdom park stage in Lake Buena Vista for renditions of his festive tunes 'Mistletoe' and 'Santa Claus is Coming to Town'. He wore white trousers and a blue military-style jacket which commanded attention while he covered every inch of the stage surrounded by an amazing team of energetic dancers popping, locking and doing head-spins. The breathtaking Disney castle was of course an incredible backdrop and the performance ended with fireworks shooting into the sky above the turrets. Biebz took time to meet fans and posed for pictures with his top dawg, Goofy.

JUSTIN BIEBER

JB wasn't travelling alone however, he brought pal Jaden Smith along for the trip and the two hung out together in Justin's downtime. Biebz tweeted photos of the pair at Vans Skate park at the Festival Bay Mall joking, "It's not about how u fall. It is about how you get back up." The pair had obviously made time to shop too, as in another shot JB and JS showed off new matching pairs of furry boots, which Biebz proclaimed to be 'swag boots'. There were also photos of Jaden's earrings – after he got his ears pierced, just like BFF Justin!

DECEMBER

Christmas with the Obamas

Isn't it typical? You are due to sing for the President of the United States and you come down with a cold! We've all been there! Well actually we haven't, but JB found himself in that exact predicament when he arrived in Washington for the Christmas in Washington Concert. The annual event raises money for the Children's National Medical Centre and is always a star-studded affair. This time the line-up included Jennifer Hudson, Victoria Justice and Cee Lo-Green but as usual JB's presence was the most highly anticipated.

Host for the evening, Conan O'Brien, poked fun at Biebz's mega-fame saying, "It's especially exciting to be here during this joyous season, when we celebrate the arrival of a miracle child, worshiped by millions around the world… Of course I'm talking about Justin Bieber." Biebz had been rough – he tweeted "Waking up with a bad cold … weather change. But will be ready tonight for CHRISTMAS in WASHINGTON. #resting,"

This must have paid off because JB looked his usual chipper self on the night in a smart black and white suit.

He performed 'Mistletoe' and joined in with the final carol 'Hark The Herald Angels Sing'. Between songs, the President spoke about the story of Jesus' birth teaching us basic values such as loving one another, keeping faith and helping those less fortunate.

Biebz had two special Beliebers in the audience the President's daughters, 13-year-old Malia and Sasha, 10. Both the girls got to meet Biebz in person as soon a the concert ended and looked like all their Christmases had come at once.

X Factor USA

Biebz is a big fan of the X Factor and was on the 1st December results show performing two songs including 'Santa Claus is coming to Town'. The star made hearts melt – even on the judging panel – when he invited 14-year-old contestant Drew, who'd just been voted off the show on stage to sing with him. Drew had stunned the judges at her audition with her amazing version of 'Baby'. Kind Biebz said, "Wait one second, I gotta do something. Drew come here" and let her sing the last line of the song before hugging her and dancing with her.

Performing with Stevie Wonder

Both Biebz performances were amazing, but his rendition of 'The Christmas Song (*Chestnut's Roasting on an Open Fire*)' was really special. In the run-up to the show, Biebz had been tweeting that there would be a surprise and some sections of the press were reporting that he would be performing '*All I Want For Christmas*' with Mariah Carey, so expectations were running high! On the night, Justin showed the would-be pop stars on the show exactly how it should be done, owning the stage in a baseball jacket with vivid green sleeves and showing off his vocal skills on the festive tune. He had been in a sole spotlight with the back of the stage in darkness, but suddenly the lights came up to reveal – not Mariah but legendary singer and musician, Stevie Wonder who joined Biebz in a duet, playing the piano and the musical break on his harmonica. The judges, Paula Abdul, Nicole Scherzinger, LA Reid and even icy Simon Cowell were all on their feet, applauding wildly!

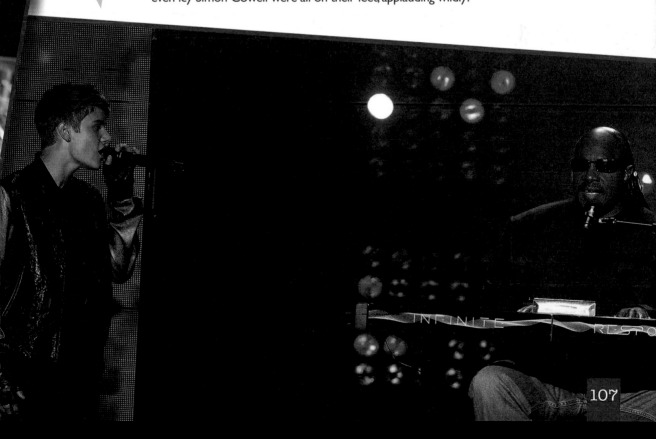

DECEMBER

NYE in Times Square

It must be hard to top a year when you've travelled across five continents, have performed to hundreds of thousands of adoring fans, met and hung with your fave sporting heroes, won countless awards and even launched your own fragrance – but Justin made sure the final night of the year was as memorable as everything else he'd done in 2011. The star performed live on Dick Clark's New Year's Rockin' Eve, presented by Ryan Seacrest, in the middle of Times Square. Lady Gaga was also on the bill although Beyoncé had to cancel as she'd gone into labour with her first baby, Blue Ivy Carter. Instead of one of his own tracks, Biebz chose to perform a song by The Beatles called 'Let It Be'. He sang the first verse on his own, seated at a white grand piano, before being joined by celebrated rock guitarist Carlos Santana. Biebz donned a bright red beanie, camel coloured coat to keep out the cold, while Santana kept warm in a Bob Marley hoodie. The Beatles' track was released back in 1970, 24 years before Justin was born but it remains a classic and the moving performance won him many, many more Beliebers.

Tweets of the month

@ Up early at The Magic Kingdom in Disney World getting ready to perform.

@ Feeling good. Just had some fun at rehearsals and now we r ready. Time to sing for the President. #canadianrepresenter.

@ Great night! President Obama is one cool Prez. He told me he was 'chillin.' #PresidentialSWAG.

@ We went real BIG on X Factor 2nite. Thank you to the legendary STEVIE WONDER and to @drewryniewicz who I hope realized dreams do come true.

@ Spending time with family - feels really good. Going to get to see these smiles on Christmas

@ Performed with Carlos Santana. Honored. #letitbe #happynewyear!

@ Thank you for 2011, lets have an even better 2012! #happynewyear.